T0334265

'This is a book that does just what the title says. In plain language, with large helpings of common sense and leavened with humour, Kursty and Neil take the reader through all the stages of developing a workspace change project, while pointing out possible pitfalls *en route*. Sharing their great expertise in such accessible form has produced a gem of a book for non-specialists and specialists alike.'

Andy Lake, *Author of* Beyond Hybrid Working *and Director of Flexibility.co.uk*

'*Workspace Made Easy* is truly a lifesaver for anyone trying to comprehend the requirements of a workspace change project, and it serves as a thorough guide to crafting functional and inspiring workspace. The book can help beginners to avoid major mistakes, and for those with experience, it can serve as a tool for improvement and better project management. The balance of providing a wealth of valuable advice while ensuring that every essential aspect receives equal attention allows the book to be comprehensive without overwhelming the reader.'

Mervi Huhtelin, *Manager, Strategic Urban Development, City of Tampere, Finland*

'*Workspace Made Easy* is the most exceptionally practical and comprehensive guide I've ever seen/read. With its foundation in real-world scenarios, careful attention to detail, and clear focus on the importance of the change process, Groves and Usher leave no stone unturned in addressing critical details often overlooked in real estate projects, from power-outlet counts to installation schedules. The book's discussion of "Change Activity" is another highlight, presenting the concept in a straightforward and easily digestible manner, in contrast to the complicated explanations found in many other resources. The consistent focus on change throughout Part III is a valuable reminder of its central role in successful real estate transformations. This book is a game-changer, ensuring success in any workspace transformation project.'

Momcilo Pavlovic, *Workplace Support Leader, Group Strategy, Development & Innovation, Ingka Group (IKEA)*

'To say *Workspace Made Easy* is a "paint by numbers" guide to workplace change would oversimplify the level of thought and detail that Kursty and Neil have gone into with this book and yet it is just that. It will take both professionals (everyone needs reminders) and novices alike on a simple journey down an often over-complicated route to creating that fantastic workspace.'

Robert Fretwell, *Space Management, Airbus UK*

'Love this book – it truly captures the full life cycle of modern workspace thinking and the changes to ways of working that businesses in their thousands are adapting to. From challenge to solution and the tools to get you there, all in one place. But most importantly, for those new to the game, those in the game and those champions you need within your business to understand the best possible outcome and delivery, this is the perfect guide for all. Ignore Kursty's and Neil's expertise at your peril. It really makes it seem so easy, and it can be if your project is delivered like this. The book's articulation of the scope of thoughts you need to consider and why is spot-on. Before my next project I will be issuing this book to my business leads to enable comprehensive, informed decisions with confidence (and to make my life easier!).'

Graeme Elliott, *Head of Workspace, Global Media & Entertainment*

'Finally! A book that simply explains the process of building a great workspace.'

Timothy Ahrensbach, *Head of Workplace Innovation, The Lego Group*

'Creating a workspace fit for the contemporary world of work is a complex and sensitive issue. Kursty and Neil have swept away those challenges with a practical and brilliantly comprehensive guide to building something magical for your team.'

Bruce Daisley, *Bestselling author of* Fortitude *and* The Joy of Work

WORKSPACE MADE EASY

Demystifying the entire workspace industry, for the non-expert and expert alike, this unique book sets out every step and consideration in how to lead a project to create a fantastic workspace.

Entirely free of baffling jargon and industry-speak, it's a refreshingly accessible, practical, down-to-earth guide applicable to all types of workspace, new or renovated and anywhere in the world. Created by two leading workspace practitioners with over half a century of combined multi-sector international experience, this book maps the process from initial idea to finished product and beyond in a succinct, logical and easy-to-follow question and answer style. It helps the reader instantly become a better project leader, and, for all those firms they'll deal with, a more informed and prepared client.

Supported by amusing and informative true stories throughout, the book is an indispensable guide that is sure to become an industry standard.

Kursty Groves is a leading workplace strategist and professor with over 25 years' experience in workspace innovation and design. Author, podcast host and international conference speaker, she's known for her insightful approach to creating inspiring work environments.

Neil Usher is an internationally experienced workplace creator and change leader with over 30 years' senior-level client-side and advisory experience. He's the author of several books, a prolific blogger and a regular speaker, known for bringing a fresh perspective while challenging assumptions and myths.

WORKSPACE MADE EASY

A clear and practical guide on
how to create a fantastic
work environment

Kursty Groves and Neil Usher

Routledge
Taylor & Francis Group

LONDON AND NEW YORK

Cover design: Papergoose

First published 2025
by Routledge
4 Park Square, Milton Park, Abingdon, Oxon OX14 4RN

and by Routledge
605 Third Avenue, New York, NY 10158

Routledge is an imprint of the Taylor & Francis Group, an informa business

British Library Cataloguing-in-Publication Data
A catalogue record for this book is available from the British Library

ISBN: 978-1-032-73201-5 (hbk)
ISBN: 978-1-032-69909-7 (pbk)
ISBN: 978-1-003-44268-4 (ebk)

DOI: 10.4324/9781003442684

Typeset in Garamond and Scala Sans
by Apex CoVantage, LLC

Contents

FULL CONTENTS

ACKNOWLEDGEMENTS

We'd like to sincerely thank Nick Brennan, Aimée Curtis, Robert Fretwell, David Humphries, Mervi Huhtelin, Eric Kerr, Andy Lake, Emma Morley, Clare Murray, Peter O'Brien, Momcilo Pavlovic, Dominic Slevin and Susan Staney for help, advice and encouragement along the way. You were amazing!

WHY THIS BOOK?

Most organisations don't move or refresh their workspace very often.

When a workspace is made ready, it's usually with the intention of it lasting for 5–10 years. Since a new workspace can cost a great deal of money and have a big effect on how people work, leading the project is an important task. Yet unless the organisation is big enough to justify the role, it's unlikely that anyone working there will have managed such a project before. So, it's likely to be given to someone who is familiar with how to manage any type of project, has the capacity to take it on, or just fancies giving it a go.

We're assuming that someone is you.

Like all fields, that which we'll term 'workplace' has its fair share of jargon and terminology that can make it difficult to understand for someone new to it. Especially when you are under time and cost pressure, facing colleagues eagerly awaiting the result, and therefore someone who needs to learn fast.

Like all fields, too, it's more complicated than we're going to explain in this book. We're offering here only what's needed to put you in a position to understand *why* some things are more complex. This book is a companion travel guide, to ensure you'll be ready for all the situations you're likely to face in creating your new workspace. You'll be able to see the direction we're heading in before you leave the house.

The amount of work we do to create workspace isn't proportional to our chances of success, but being smart about it is. Workspace rarely – if ever – succeeds or fails *in total*. The success of a workspace exists in a fluid state over time along a spectrum from roaring success to utter failure. Even more likely, different parts of the workspace will be at different points on the spectrum at different times.

Before we dive in, a couple of clarifications on the use of the term 'workspace' are needed.

First, we've used the term 'workspace' instead of both 'office' and 'workplace' wherever possible unless there's a compelling reason otherwise. So, you'll still see 'office' and 'workplace' pop up occasionally, as needed. 'Office' is more generally understood to be the building itself rather than the working environment within. 'Workplace' can include many other things beyond physical space, such as organisational structures and culture, processes, technologies and futures. As important as those matters can be, we're only focussed in this book on physical workspace.

Second, we've used the term 'workspace' because we feel what we've set out goes beyond 'office' or 'knowledge worker' environments and may apply to many different settings such as studios, laboratories, workshops and the like.

We'd like to suggest that, if this is your first project creating or changing workspace, you read the book right through before you begin. It's important to see where the whole journey might lead – where you are, where you're heading and how you're going to get there. It's rarely explained in this way to anyone new to the field. Thereafter, it may be worth keeping it handy when you get things (or the project) under way.

Arriving at the optimum sequence of events has been a challenge. As with many fields, those familiar with the way things work often have the confidence to complete tasks simultaneously or to take short cuts that someone new to it may not. So, if you already have experience in creating a new workspace, we appreciate that you may have a different view on the order in which we've set out the steps. Regardless, we'd like to suggest that the book could act as a handy *aide memoir* if you have run a project or two in the past – especially as it takes into account recent shifts since the Covid-19 pandemic.

As you can probably imagine, behind this short book there are a significant number of what we might call 'pro-tools'. It would have been tempting to throw them all in, in a vain attempt to look smart. But we've tried to keep things as simple as possible and give you what you need to understand your business needs and work better with any professional advisers you may choose to engage. Of course, if you need anything, just ask! Our contact details can be found below.

There are also numerous processes, certifications and accreditations related to the creation and operation of workspace in every country. New ones are appearing all the time. It would be impossible to include them all; any listing we'd cite would soon be out of date. This is an area best left to a professional team to advise on, depending on the scope of your project and organisational priorities.

If you're keen to explore more, there are plenty of excellent books and podcasts about the wider workplace available that are more detailed, analytical and academic than this book. There's a role for them all in developing a broader understanding of our craft together. We've offered a list of further reading at the end.

While there are many methods, processes and techniques that workplace professionals and practitioners use, we feel that there are a few basic tools that can help get you started. We've created some free templates and checklists to help you organise your planning, research and data collection to make it easier for you to define, design and create your new workspace. You'll find them at www.workspace-made-easy.com.

In the meantime, we hope you enjoy reading our book and that you find it useful. We've certainly enjoyed writing it, and we'd be delighted if it's noticeable. We love what we do.

There's nothing quite like seeing colleagues loving the outcome. Whether you've completed one project or a hundred, that feeling never goes away. It remains for us to wish you the best of luck with creating your new workspace – if you feel inclined, please share your story with us; we'd love to hear about your journey!

Kursty and Neil, 2024

If you wish to get in contact:

Kursty

X:	@kurstyg
LinkedIn:	linkedin.com/in/kursty
Instagram:	instagram.com/kurstyg
Email:	kursty@shapeworklife.com

Neil

X:	@workessence
LinkedIn:	linkedin.com/in/neilusher
Instagram:	instagram.com/w0rkessence
Email:	neilusher@hotmail.com

TRUE STORIES

In the course of their work, the authors are constantly asked for examples and case studies to support what they advise, whether it be things done well or situations where they weren't. In over half a century of combined experience in the discipline, naturally we've collected anecdotes. Throughout the book, therefore, we've included stories of real-life incidents or situations that support the points being made. The names of the organisations and people have been removed out of respect. We hope you find them useful – or, in some cases perhaps, simply entertaining.

PART I

WHAT DO WE NEED AND WHY?

1

CHECK-IN
WHERE ARE WE NOW?

Before we do anything, we'll need to consider the broader post-pandemic context we're operating in and how this relates specifically to our workspace needs.

WORKSPACE – ARE WE SURE WE NEED IT?

Yes, we're doing this.

Until the Covid-19 pandemic of 2020–2021, 'work' for the billion or so 'knowledge workers' worldwide was generally considered to be synonymous with the office. 'Going to work' meant travelling to a workspace, Monday through Friday, to fulfil contractual hours… and probably, quite often more.

Seismic shifts in connectivity, hardware and mobile technology had made working-from-anywhere possible for knowledge and process workers since the 1990s. Yet before the global pandemic, only a small minority of organisations embraced this to any degree, the key problem being a lack of trust at leadership level that any work would get done from anywhere but the office.

DOI: 10.4324/9781003442684-2

But throughout the pandemic, during several 'lockdowns', work *did* get done – in many cases, more work than once had in the office with its many distractions. At the same time, for those working from home, the absence of the often expensive, unpleasant and time-consuming commute helped create an improved balance of work and personal life.

As a result, many people moved away from cities, while organisations stepped up location-independent recruitment, the outcome for some being a far more dispersed workforce. The number of 'distributed' (also known as 'location agnostic or 'remote-first') organisations exploded, with some new companies starting up without workspaces at all. Many others gave theirs up altogether. Media chatter heralded the 'death of the office', as the logic of shepherding droves of people to the same place at the same time every day finally unravelled.

During the pandemic, apart from those who needed to be present full-time by virtue of their role or for practical reasons, we learned that:

- Task-related work can often, given the right physical environment, happen away from an office, and we can connect digitally whenever we need …

BUT

- Coordination and cooperation sometimes benefit from 'quality' time with colleagues physically together, in the same place – essentially to review stuff that's been done and to plan what needs to happen next. The sort of things that after we've met, we think: 'Imagine trying to do that over a call or e-mail!'
- Exploratory and strategic work is sometimes better done 'in real life' (IRL) – especially when sharing tacit information, or tackling tricky or sensitive problems.
- Coaching, mentoring, culture, relationship-building and the pastoral (caring) aspects of work can often benefit from face-to-face interaction.

Of course, none of the above are hard-and-fast rules and are always context dependent. They also represent a prevailing view formed from the pandemic experience.

This all has led to **hybrid working** becoming the norm for many once office-based organisations, with people spending part of their time at home, and part in their organisation's workspace. Exactly how this works for each is still the subject of much experimentation and in some cases contention.

In this context, the wider landscape continues to be one of rich and often animated debate about the benefits of being alone, being together for some of the time, and being together all the time. While much remains unresolved and is likely to stay this way for some time, we have established that while the office isn't dead, what we need from it is different.

While it would be fascinating to explore the trends in more depth, for the purposes of this project and our organisation, we're assuming the decision is that we're having workspace, that's not in question. The aim is to create the best possible workspace for our needs.

WHAT IS HYBRID WORKING?

As it's quite likely we'll incorporate some form of hybrid working, it's worth spending a little time to understand it. There's much confusion over its definition, the word 'hybrid' often used interchangeably with 'flexible' and 'agile'. We can simply express these terms as follows:

- **Flexible**: *when* we work – the days of the week and times of day.
- **Hybrid**: *where* we work – meaning home or office, usually assigned to a primary corporate location. Where there are several location options, it's been called 'work from anywhere'.
- **Agile**: *how* we work – systems, processes, technologies, organisational and managerial structures.

We can think of these three aspects of a role as the 'trinity of work'. It's expected, naturally, that organisations may have developed different definitions of the three terms – but this is how each shall be used in this book.

For each characteristic, there's a spectrum on which we can mark each job role. Industry norms and organisational culture will influence where each sit on the spectrum.

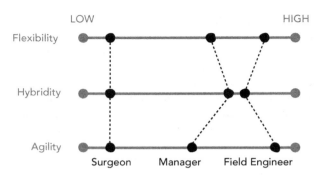

Figure 1.1 Typical roles on the 'trinity of work' spectrum.

Neither 'end' of the spectrum is superior to the other. High flexibility, hybridity and agility doesn't necessarily mean higher paid or more important! For example, a specialist surgeon may have a strict rota, work on-site at a hospital, and need to follow rigid and established procedures. Or, a field engineer might work a flexible schedule, in or out of the office depending on work demands and be free to define their approach to problems as they arise.

A typical metropolitan, office-based, middle management role when plotted on the spectrum might look something like the diagram in Figure 1.1, while the surgeon would be close to the three left-hand blobs, and the field engineer would be closer to the right three.

These are far from absolute in most cases, but more a general guide to illustrate. It's possible that our surgeon may have online patient calls, work at several clinics, meet with suppliers offsite for lunch and write up case notes in their home office. Our field engineer may have a very strict set of operating procedures and appointments and have little leeway in how they operate. You get the idea.

WHY MIGHT WE NEED HYBRID WORKING?

Hybrid working can have several advantages for individuals, teams and the organisation, including:

- **Delineation** between work and home life, giving a greater sense of personal control and balance, (assuming the individual has the permission to delineate).

- Reduced **cost** of the daily commute for five days a week.
- Commute **time** can be reassigned to productive, task-related activity or personal time.
- Work can happen in the appropriate **setting**.
- It takes advantage of available **technology**.

Yet several problems remain unresolved to date with hybrid working:

- The **necessity** of face-to-face (F2F) work with colleagues is still challenged by some, who see even hybrid working as impacting freedom of choice.
- Where face-to-face work is required, it may yield **scheduling** challenges, (logistics, time and effort), in needing to be in the workspace at the same time.
- Irregular attendance schedules don't benefit people with regular and important **personal** responsibilities (children, caring etc).
- Being in the workspace less often (and thus less 'seen') can affect **recognition** and **career** advancement prospects (often called 'proximity bias').
- The 'post-pandemic pinch' creates **capacity** challenges. Reducing the number of days people need to be in the workspace drives a surge in attendance midweek. This, in turn, presents the problem of sustaining a workspace large enough to support busy days, but that lies near empty at other times.
- Misinterpretation or abuse of loose **guidelines** can result in double-standards, and a reaction against the implementation of new hybrid practices. To regulate (and in some cases, understand) how it works, we've seen an increase in rulemaking and a descent into rotas, shifts and meaningless mandates. With flexibility comes great responsibility.
- Where organisations impose mandated or strongly recommended attendance guidelines, **enforcement** creates challenges (not least, considerable workload) regarding both data collection and practice, which in turn creates negative sentiment.

TRUE STORY

An organisation was formulating its hybrid working strategy during the pandemic, ready for the eventual easing of 'social distancing'. They were keen not to be too prescriptive, and to allow free choice for teams of how often to get together in their (excellent) workspace. During planning, a question was asked during a 'town hall' as to what the minimum attendance might be. 'We'd like to see you once a month' was the answer from the HR director. As a result, most teams arranged their own face-to-face meeting once a month. Colleagues who came to the workspace more regularly complained about a lack of energy and life. Colleagues who attended team meetings complained that they only ever saw the same few people within the organisation. We have to be so careful about what we say, when and how.

Designing, implementing and sustaining a hybrid working programme must be intentional, it's not just a case of declaring it and hoping for the best. Therefore, it needs to be carefully designed and operated, reviewed and refined. The approach will typically be one of the following, each of which has advantages and disadvantages:

1   **Free choice** of when to attend, with no constraints.
2   A **recommended** number of days to be present in the workspace. This can be positioned as specific team or organisational **anchor days** during a week, or a percentage of time over a longer period such as a month or quarter. For some organisations, the recommended time together might be at locations other than the workspace.
3   A firm **mandate** requiring attendance for a given number of days or specific days.

Despite its popularity, there's much still to learn about hybrid working practice. Developing a hybrid working strategy is not within the scope of this book. Our job here is to create a fantastic workspace that enables people to work within it for as long as they need, when they need, and with whom they need– and enjoy doing so! Later in Part I we'll consider how much workspace we'll need, which will factor in the extent to which we're hybrid working.

WHAT DO WE NEED OUR WORKSPACE FOR?

Workspace plays a role for different audiences, and so there may be many reasons why it's needed. Here are some, noting that these tasks may be performed remotely at times, too.

Intentional requirements (as in, those related to a specific purpose or to perform specific tasks). For the organisation, and its customers and partners:

- Legal and statutory (an office is required in a territory)
- Sales and demonstration
- Staging and training
- Support and aftercare
- Research and development (R&D)
- Siting technology and equipment
- Business events (presentations, all-hands gatherings, town halls etc)
- Storage
- Crisis response.

For the organisation's employees:

- Individual focussed work (including catering for those with no practical alternative)
- Teamwork – company, conversation, coordination and cooperation
- Planned exploration and collaboration
- Meetings
- Case work, involving 1:1 consultation
- Human resources tasks (recruitment, interviewing, disciplinary)
- Learning and training
- Conducting research and development
- Accessing technology and equipment
- Accessing stored materials or resources
- Social contact with colleagues

- Social events
- A place in which to feel 'at work'.

Byproducts of being there (as in, outcomes not related to a specific purpose):

- Unplanned exploration and collaboration
- Meeting new people
- Developing relationships
- Connecting with a sense of common purpose
- Motivation and energy
- Informal learning and awareness
- Secondment to projects or initiatives
- Career development
- Informal or unplanned social activities.

As byproducts, they mostly don't arise unless we're there for the intentional, task-related requirements. It's not to say that the byproducts aren't possible without a workspace, but they may occur less frequently or take a different form.

WHAT TYPES OF WORK WILL WE DO IN OUR WORKSPACE?

As the discussion of why we need a workspace suggests, all 'office work' is not the same. Workspace will essentially need to cater for two types:

- **Task work**: where people know what they need to do and who they need to do it with, using existing processes and technology. It's the work people are hired and paid for; the core job description. In carrying out task work, we either work alone or we coordinate and cooperate with colleagues. The outcome is known as productivity. Much of this work can be done anywhere that suits the individual or team.
- **Exploratory work**: not working to instructions but exploring possibilities out of curiosity with colleagues from other teams. Sometimes it's planned, (as in the case of strategy sessions and

creative workshops), but it's often accidental. The outcome is unknown, often yielding nothing immediately. When it does lead to something, it's understood as innovation. Exploratory work requires the building of trust over time, and therefore often benefits from people being physically together from time-to-time.

As ideas are explored and more colleagues become involved in turning them into a reality, exploratory work evolves into planned and intentional task work.

We'll come back to these ideas as the book progresses, as we'll need to think about planning our space accordingly.

THINGS TO LOOK OUT FOR

Here are some of the things to look out for in this area, to challenge or avoid wherever possible. The themes of this chapter are probably more written and talked about than any other. Filters on, here goes for a summary:

- **'The office is dead!'** Just as there's always someone prophesising the end of the world on a city street corner, so there'll always be someone telling us the office is all over bar the demolition. As discussed at the start of this chapter, it's clearly not (at least in our case), but we have no means of taking its blood pressure and running some scans. So, we need to see how it changes in purpose and shape from here. The pendulum swung from 'everyone in' to 'everyone home' during the pandemic and is starting to swing the other way again. It's yet to find an equilibrium, but when it does, the office will feature in some form, wherever it settles.
- **Hybrid working** – where to begin? There are those who love the expression and those who think we should ban it from workplace lexicon; those who think it's the best thing to ever happen to work, those who see inequality and frustration; those who think it's here to stay, and those who think it's a passing fad and we'll all be back to the office/working from home forever. From every angle, polarisation. The simple

matter is, we're all still learning what it means in practice and how to make it work best.

- **'All work can be done at home/in the office'** (delete as you prefer). Work isn't all the same, and so the places we do it in, and who we do it with, are part of the challenge we face in determining what workspace we need. Thus, a slightly deeper understanding of how work happens within the organisation is vital.

2

UNDERSTAND
WHAT HAVE WE GOT?

*With our context understood, we'll now need to get clear on our starting point –
the knowledge, resources and assets we have available, and where the gaps are.*

WHAT'S OUR TRIGGER?

The chances are that something has either happened or is about
to happen that's sparked the need to change our workspace.
The trigger can come from internal or external factors, or a
combination of both. It's worth understanding what's behind
the need for change because it'll shape everything from our
vision to the outcome. It'll drive our approach, timing and
budget.

The trigger might be any of the following:

- **Things have changed**: in our environment, markets, interests, it could be anything, anywhere – even a pandemic – but
  it's prompted us to realise that the space we're working in isn't
  right any longer. It's possible we can't quite put our finger on

DOI: 10.4324/9781003442684-3

why at this stage. We just feel it. And we wish to set about discovering why, and what we need to do.

- **We want to change**: either considered as a positive response, in that as an organisation we can see what 'better' looks like and aspire to be there; or as a response to something negative, for example, we realise that something is amiss or out of alignment culturally and needs to change. In both instances our workspace is seen as being a key part of that journey, either for how it appears to our people and/or customers, how it works or how it supports our people in their work.

- A Real Estate '**event**' (as they're often called): as in, contractually we must decide. It's usually the end of, or a formal break in, a commercial property lease. If all is well and we're happy with the space we have, we may opt to stay and extend the lease, if permissible. But it's usually a good time to think about doing something differently if that's an option. The vital thing with a lease break is to make sure the exact terms of the (lease) agreement are understood well in advance to ensure it's not missed.

- **Growth**: either organic, through an innovation, or through a merger or acquisition – we're bigger than we were before and have outgrown our workspace. In which case we probably only noticed when the space didn't fit anymore and so we're already feeling frustrated. There'll likely be a 'straw breaking the camel's back' moment.

- **Contraction**: either because the organisation, for whatever reason, is getting smaller or it has concerns that the workspace is costing too much. In the post-pandemic world, it's become common with the move of most organisations to hybrid working for the penny to finally drop that 'less but better' (an approach encapsulated in the work of industrial designer Dieter Rams) workspace is required. It can be argued that this was achievable pre-pandemic for many, but that it wasn't deemed a priority.

- **Envy:** someone else has done something better. Likely a competitor. Suddenly the organisation looks like the laggard of the sector and is dealing with a forecast of a mass exodus of talent, even its demise. A question often asked at the early stages of a workspace project is: 'What are our competitors doing?' It always feels like the wrong question, as an organisation should focus on what's right for them and their people. But it's useful nonetheless, to know, as industry sectors often share a talent pool.

TRUE STORY

A client was adamant they needed a campus. A dynamic, fast-expanding business, they saw it as the way to optimise their culture (which they espoused 'ate strategy for breakfast'). They'd even instructed workspace designers to start imagining it. But they didn't have a strategy to eat. So, we ran a 'strategy sprint' for 2 weeks, to show the executive team the power of understanding what was needed. It transpired that what they really wanted was to be together under one roof, to enable culture building and fast decision-making. The campus idea quietly disappeared.

With each of the above, leadership impatience will come as standard. With the creation of a new workspace, there's a lot at stake. The last thing we should tell someone who wants something to have happened yesterday is 'don't rush' – but don't rush. We can move through the process quickly, but we must resist the urge to skip steps. Work done at this early stage lays a solid foundation for what's to come. Our future selves will thank us.

WHY ARE WE HERE?

We must be both historian and archaeologist to discover the trail that led to today, in terms of both property and people. Establishing our baseline is vital. If we don't invest the time and energy at this stage, mistakes will happen, even the same ones as last time, and possibly expensive ones.

However crazy our current situation may seem, when it comes to our workspace, there was always a rational reason for us being where we are. Yet it's rare in most organisations that history is laid out neatly, even if we were part of its making. Where once we looked back through paper files to make sense of the past, organisations today rarely organise their digital knowledge in such a transparent way. Often, knowledge walks out of the door with the people who leave.

The information we're seeking comes in two forms: **data** (head) and **story** (heart). Together, they make information more clear and compelling: data gives story credibility; story makes data interesting.

- **Data**: information that's logical, numerical, concrete, rational and objective. Hard, irrefutable facts. This type of information is well within the comfort zone of most organisations. Interestingly, while it's unlikely we'd ever get a decision from leadership without it, direction is often given by leadership in its absence. The more junior we are the more vulnerable, and so the more data is required.
- **Story**: when we're dealing with human beings, the life blood of organisations – imperfect, changeable, emotional, irrational, creatures that make organisations unique – we're in the realm of story. The information we gather from and about the organisation's people is more subjective, attitudinal, and difficult to quantify.

The combination helps us build a full picture of what's going on in the organisation and allows us to fully understand what the organisation and its people need. Even, as is often the case, they don't' know it yet.

Let's start with the 'hard' data.

PROPERTY AND WORKSPACE – WHAT HAVE WE GOT?

There are six key items we can crack on with gathering (or if necessary, creating) at this stage. We'll need them all at some point soon, so it's never wasted time:

- We'll need our property **lease** and any other contractual documentation, particularly that which relates to our obligations in respect of either staying or going. Leases are often written in 'legalese' and so we may need an expert to translate it for us.

- The lease will also inform us of the extent, process and timing related to what are called **dilapidations**, or the requirement to return the workspace to an agreed condition upon leaving. This may even be all the way back to the original condition when the organisation first moved in, and so any records of this will be needed. It's often worth looking for this documentation as early as possible – it's all too common that they've evaporated somewhere along the line. Negotiating dilapidations will usually need specialist help, but the fees are very often recovered several times over in the savings they can achieve against a landlord's initial claim.
- **Space plans** are usually drawn in AutoCAD or similar software. It's still very much a manual process. If they don't exist, they can be created by a design or project management firm, but it'll require a space survey and can take up to several weeks to organise and complete. If space plans do exist, and we can find them, they're rarely current and so will need to be updated.
- An understanding how many of each of the key **worksettings** we have – especially desks and meeting rooms, will be helpful. They can be counted from space plans and an accompanying spreadsheet created, including type, quantity and seats or positions in each. With any new workspace proposal, we'll often be asked how it compares to the existing workspace.
- An **inventory** of furniture and IT equipment (desktop kit and audio visual, usually) will be needed that might be re-used in the new workspace. This will help with budgeting. A full, unquestioned turnover of everything is not often compatible with the environmental aims of most organisations or societies and can be perceived negatively.
- Occasionally, alongside a lease there may be **social** commitments – promises the organisation has made to the community – that may be compromised by relocating. A knowledge of the history is vital here, as it's unlikely that the property lease will mention them. Conversations with long-standing colleagues or neighbours can be a quick way to uncover this information.

We may wish to avoid widely circulating the information and data collected at this stage beyond those who may need to act on it in future, until we've developed our vision and objectives. The next chapter refers to why this might be advisable.

At this stage, using this information it would be helpful for our key stakeholders to create an early analysis of **risks** and **opportunities**.

- For **risks**, we might set out each and describe a mitigation or removal strategy. A sophisticated risk analysis might include as assessment of frequency (how often it might happen), likelihood (of it happening) and severity (how bad it would be if it happens). It's likely that for now, it won't need to be this granular.
- For **opportunities**, we might describe each and add an optimisation strategy – that is, how we can make the most of what is presented.

It's a tool that can be updated and developed throughout the project.

ORGANISATION AND PEOPLE – WHO HAVE WE GOT?

There are four key areas on which we need to focus at this stage, all of which are related, to understand who is in scope for our new workspace:

- An organisational map, or **organigram**, of how each of the key units or teams fits together to form the whole. Like an organisation chart, but with teams and departments. Everyone working with us will need to know who's who and how the organisation is structured. We may have to create it, as they don't always exist. It can be a valuable activity that can help the organisation to understand itself.

- It's beneficial at this stage to also understand key **team relationships** – who works with who. While during the pandemic we became very accomplished at working within our teams and developing existing relationships, inter-team relationships in some cases suffered. There's likely to be some relevance to the organigram – at least as a starter. Sometimes they won't align at all. We can only discover these relationships through talking to the right colleagues. By merging the organigram with existing and emerging relationships across the organisation, a new picture may emerge of important links not captured elsewhere.
- From our organigram, it's essential to create a **people database**, a single version of the truth. It will cover everyone that in principle will be attached to and use – at some time – our new workspace. This is often left till far too late in a workspace project but is ideally needed now for:
  - Requirements planning – in particular, the amount of space needed
  - Distribution lists, for project communication
  - IT kit and services
  - Move management.
- It's likely to be in spreadsheet form and as a minimum it'll have:
  - First name
  - Family name
  - Role title
  - Department
  - Team
  - E-mail
  - Contracted place of work
  - Usual place of work (not always the above in the era of hybrid working)
  - Location (building/floor).
- The nature of the information collected may mean there are **data privacy** issues, depending on the country in which the project is taking place. We'll need to speak with the relevant

expert within the organisation to understand what can and can't be done with the data.

- From our people database, we need to understand who is likely to use our workspace: our **attendee model**. The total number will be vital for our requirements planning. We'll have 'Residents' – those in our people database, whether they attend or not, who have a right to be there – and if we have more than one location, we may also have:
  o Regular attendees: if we have more than one location, those who aren't attached to our workspace but are there (say) 4–6 times a month.
  o Occasional attendees: those who aren't attached to our workspace but are there (say) 1–2 times a month.
  o Other colleagues, who may attend infrequently, or never be there.

Creating an attendee model

Considering our Residents, for those workspaces where daily attendance is expected or mandated, this will be a straightforward process.

For hybrid workspaces where a degree of choice is permitted, they'll fall into one of the below four categories, see Figure 2.1:

- **Daily**: 4–5 days, the workspace as a regular place of work, from any of:
  o Necessity: it's not possible to work at home
  o The nature of the role
  o Preference
  o Organisational requirement or mandate.
- **Weekly**: 1–2 days a week for coordination and cooperation with colleagues. Regular attendees from other sites would fall into this category.
- **Monthly**: 1–2 days a month, as a means of maintaining a degree of visibility and connection. Occasional attendees from other sites would fall into this category.
- **Never**: either based in a physically remote location, or whose role has no necessity to be present for any reason.

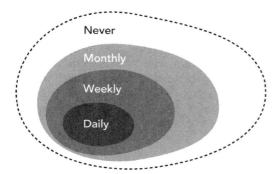

Figure 2.1 Frequency of attendance.

It's recommended that we create an **attendee (or potential usage) model** to arrive at our estimated number of attendees and reconcile this against our utilisation data (covered below). This model would need to be based on expressed intent, so we'll need to ask each team to identify which of their people fall into which of the four categories. It will helpfully reflect where people live, an important consideration post-pandemic. Daily and weekly attendees will likely count as 1, monthly as 0.5 and never as 0. If we have multiple sites with an expectation of attendance at our new workspace, whether 'regular' or 'occasional', we'll need to ask those teams, too.

We'll need to be prepared to challenge some responses if they don't appear right. Pre-pandemic, there was often a tendency for colleagues to over-estimate space needed or attendance levels, but this approximation bias now varies depending on the leaning of the respondent toward their preferred place of work.

We also need to take into consideration in what we might term **natural absence**, which accounts for holidays, sickness, training, events, working at other locations and schedule changes, and usually reduces our total by around 10%.

This will give us an effective **attendee number** that we'll use to calculate or space requirement, covered below.

Of course, our potential usage model assumes attendance is evenly distributed throughout the week; this is hardly ever the case without intervention. But at this stage, for the purposes of establishing a starting estimation, this is sufficient. Rather than attempting to model complex weekly patterns, we'll likely (depending on the organisation's hybrid working strategy) be engaging in initiatives to try and distribute attendance more evenly in due course.

HOW ARE WE USING OUR WORKSPACE TODAY?

It's essential to know how the workspace is being used today, as well as what's working and what's not, to form a baseline of knowledge for our future workspace. Information typically collected usually consists of three types:

Space utilisation

As referenced above, this is a measure of some or all the following, either as a 'point in time' snapshot or as a trend over time:

- How many people are **attending** the workspace every day: either from security gate data, sensors (under-desk type or ceiling-mounted cameras, bought or rented) or visual observation.
- What areas or worksettings they are **using** while there: from sensors or visual observation.
- What they're **doing** while there: visual observation only.

Gathering detailed utilisation data manually is labour intensive and expensive, and, given the irregular patters of attendance post-pandemic, is now for the most part obsolete.

Before gathering this data, notification will need to be given to everyone within the workspace detailing the extent of the data being collected, and the purpose in doing so. That is, to understand how the workspace is being used to inform a better design in future. Assurances of anonymity will likely be required.

TRUE STORY

An organisation collected security gate data as part of determining its requirements for a relocation. It established that of around 1,250 people allocated to its workspace, average daily attendance post-pandemic was around 300. Their 'hybrid' approach was based solely on free choice, with team leaders able to exercise discretion. One of the authors was later brought into the project to work on change and communications and asked whether the 300 or so attendees were the *same* 300. As in, how many of the 1,250 never attended at all? This question hadn't been asked at the strategy stage. Yet it was the critical question, both in terms of planning and engagement. In gathering data, we have to ask the right questions.

Visual observation

Using a method loved by anthropologists, who take a much longer-term view of data and insight gathering than may be possible here, time can be spent in the existing workspace noting:

- Who is working where.
- Who is doing what, and how.
- What worksettings are working and used, and what aren't.
- What problems and inconveniences people are confronting.
- Where conversations are happening, and for how long.
- General mood and demeanour in the workspace.

The observations can be in the form of notes and photos.

As with utilisation studies, notice should be given that this is happening, especially where photos are being taken. Consent may be required by those appearing in the photos for their use in any report or presentation.

Satisfaction survey

The world of workplace relies heavily on surveys in the absence of other meaningful data collection tools. Such surveys seek to understand things such as:

- Levels of satisfaction with the existing workspace overall.
- Levels of satisfaction with specific features of the existing workspace.
- Which features or services are of most importance today.
- What additional features or services might be required in future.
- Anything else of importance or note (free text).

They have several benefits:

- It's **data** – even if qualitative and subjective – and likely to be valued by colleagues and leaders alike. It's the 'voice of the people'.
- As an **established** technique, they're a useful, simple and low cost means of gauging sentiment to which everyone can relate.
- It's vital that any workspace **reflects the views**, feelings and needs of its occupants. During the change process the 'you said – we did' approach is often very powerful, as the features of our new workspace can be tracked back to what was asked for at the time of the survey. Noting that this process isn't 'order taking', rather it acts as useful information.
- They allow for a **controlled expression** of opinion, however strongly felt, rather than the more random and destructive expression that can be found in internal and external social channels.
- We can use a survey to conduct an **early test** of opinion on certain intended features or amenities of our new workspace, and the types of desired behaviour we'd like to see.

Care is needed over what conclusions are derived from them, for several reasons:

- They're a **point-in-time** event. Timing is often everything. Releasing it the day after an announcement of redundancies in the middle of a severe Winter will likely skew the results. Or releasing it straight after three other unrelated surveys, leading to a low response rate – what's known as 'survey fatigue'.
- The **response rate** can be low. Anything below 50% won't give us a well-informed picture, so care should be taken to keep surveys relevant and easy to complete. In some cases, existing 'pulse' surveys can form good platforms for adding space-related questions, so a conversation with our HR colleagues may help us to design something that's useful and appropriate.

- They can sometimes be **heart** masquerading as **head**, in that numbers are put to opinions. Colleague sentiment, while very valid and important, needs to be treated as such. And very often, quotes from one or two articulate colleagues can often provide as much insight as a large number of 'satisfied' responses to a standardised question.
- They won't inform as to **why** something is the case, just that it is. Including the option for colleagues to respond with their own comments means they can be analysed for themes and patterns. However, we must allow time to fully process and synthesise this valuable information; a 'word cloud' doesn't count in this regard, and although there are a number of free processing applications, the output is often sketchy at best.

It's easy to create what's needed in free or low-cost survey tools. There are several ready-made tools on the market, which allow for benchmarking with other organisations and workspaces.

TRUE STORY

A large organisation ran an annual workspace satisfaction survey. Top of the list were always: not enough desks, meeting rooms or car parking spaces. Every year, the committed and hardworking FM team seemed stuck in a perpetual cycle of shuffling floorplates and mandating stricter rules. When the advisory team ran some observational studies, invaluable insights were revealed: meeting rooms were often booked but unused due to a habit of block booking up to six months ahead; around 10% of the floor space was taken up by filing cabinets that weren't used or accessed at all in over 16 weeks; three car parking spaces were given over to a container housing paperwork that hadn't been touched in over three years; and people were observed gathering around scraps of wall space to share project information. None of these insights were revealed by the survey that simply asked how satisfied people were with meeting and desk availability. Sometimes we have to dig much deeper, keep our eyes open and keep asking 'why?'.

WHAT WORKS AND WHAT DOESN'T?

While data collection may indicate where people tend to spend their time while in the workspace and whether they're happy with it, it doesn't give any depth of insight. For this, we need to talk to people. Either in the form of one-to-one interviews, focus groups, people watching, or all of the above.

Understanding the gap between what people say they want and our visual observations around what they currently do (and how they do it) may provide some rich ground for new solutions.

It's always best to take a 'horizontal' and 'vertical' cut through the organisation when deciding who to include – as in, a broad spectrum of roles (customer-facing and support) and seniority (not just leaders and managers).

A useful structure for such conversations is the 'keep, ditch, create' approach:

- **Keep**: what's working – there's always something that is, that colleagues won't want to lose.
- **Ditch**: what's not working – which is often more than is considered to be working!
- **Create**: what's needed that we don't have today. It doesn't matter if this gets fanciful, the chocolate fountain is unlikely to make the cut but does hint at a desire for more social interaction. (Always remember the golden question: 'why?').

We may be able to undertake these sessions ourselves, but while there's no rocket science involved, it's helpful to obtain an independent, unbiased view.

We've now got a good understanding of what we have, who is included and what our colleagues are thinking. We're ready to start defining what we want from our new workspace.

THINGS TO LOOK OUT FOR

Here are some of the things to look out for in this area, to challenge or avoid wherever possible.

- **Copy + paste**: 'We just need to copy something we've seen that we like.' A few minutes of searching online can create quite an inferiority complex. But we must remember that the photos we see are curated, often taken before anyone has moved in, sometimes before IT kit is installed, and can present an unreal picture of the workspace. The photos also won't tell us if the workspace is working for the occupants, or if the ways of working have changed from the previous workspace. Sometimes a picture can be worth no words at all. Searching for inspiration is great, but simply copying doesn't guarantee success.

- **Cool workspace = happy people**: 'Unless we have a cool workspace, everyone will leave and no-one will want to join.' While the pandemic showed us that people won't bother trekking into a workspace that doesn't work, 'cool' isn't always the solution. It depends entirely on what and who we need it for. Fads and fashions pass, and today's idea of cool may well be embarrassing tomorrow.

- **We know what we want**: 'We don't need data or to ask our colleagues, we know what we want.' It may be because (as above) there's an intent to copy and paste a cool workspace seen elsewhere. Boldness and courage are often admired in leaders when it comes to making decisions – but it can make a mockery of collecting data or engaging with people on what they may want and closes the possibility of dialogue. We need to be open to new ideas and approaches – the stuff we don't know we don't know.

- **Experts have all the answers**: 'We need workspace designers to tell us what we're doing wrong and what we need.' We don't. It's the opposite problem of the point above. What workspace strategists and designers *can* do is show us the art of the possible, the stuff we don't know exists. They can tell us how other clients have solved problems we may be encountering. But we can start understanding ourselves by ourselves. Which means when it comes to selecting strategists and designers, we'll be more assured and confident in our search.

3

DEFINE
WHAT DO WE WANT?

We've established our context, together with the knowledge, resources and assets we have and need – now the shaping begins: our vision, objectives, space required and type of workspace.

WHAT'S OUR VISION?

Many of our colleagues will have a vision of what the new workspace should be like – probably without realising it's different from everyone else's. To understand what we really need from our workspace we need to begin to align the influencers and decision-makers. This means talking about it.

Since our workspace will be a response to how we work, it's equally essential that we need to think about not just how we work today (as covered in chapter 1), but also how we may – or would like – to work tomorrow. If we build for what we do today, it could be out of date in a year.

In doing so, we must deal with the age-old problem which we referred to in the last chapter: not knowing what we don't know.

DOI: 10.4324/9781003442684-4

That is, being restricted in our view of what we think we'd like in future by what we have today. Like Henry Ford saying if he asked people what they wanted, they'd have said 'faster horses'. For instance, if we've never seen a cafe in a workspace acting as a reception area, we may not envision it because we don't know it's possible.

We'll also need to acknowledge that our visioning may be impacted by the unexpected, such as the rapid emergence of generative AI, or seismic societal events such as the Covid-19 pandemic.

All of which means getting out and about and doing some research is a good place to start. Although, as we've already cautioned, this doesn't mean simply copying others.

If we decide to engage with workplace strategists or interior architects (the latter being a term we've used to also mean workplace designer, as we'll explain in Part II) we'll benefit from involving them in this stage of the project. They can help us to identify what's possible, research examples of other workspaces that may be interesting as well as present workspace design trends. However, an advantage of undertaking this work ourselves is that our research may introduce us to a range of advisers and experts, which may help us find those who understand and align with our vision.

We may get the opportunity to co-create both the vision and objectives (covered next) with senior leadership (whether alone or with some of our professional team), or we may have to create a draft ourselves from conversations, then table them for comment and approval.

Our decision regarding *when* to define the vision might vary, depending on the current level of engagement from senior leaders and the extent to which they're aligned. There's a compelling argument for defining what we need **before** reviewing what we have. Particularly when we anticipate that we'll need to stretch or align the perspectives or views of some colleagues. We can sometimes become restricted by an in-depth knowledge of the present, unable to imagine a future that responds to how we'd like to be. Or, at least, to restrict access to the information collated on where we are today to those who will need to act on it later, rather than making it widely known at this point.

HOW SHOULD WE FRAME OUR VISION?

Our vision needs to be the one statement or question that stays with us throughout the project, from which everything flows and against which every decision can be tested. It needs to have a few key characteristics:

- **Why?** This project must be worthwhile doing, and we must be able to put our finger firmly on the reason. It should be linked clearly to the mission or vision of the organisation – which means finding out what that is, if we don't already know. It must be something that makes us want to stop doing what we're doing and do this instead, which means it must fizz with excitement.
- **How?** We must be able to get there, practically and financially. It should also be in-line with our values – the *way* we go about transforming and running our workspace should reflect how stuff happens here.
- **What?** We must be able to understand the place we're trying to get to and what our workspace will enable us to achieve – even if at this stage we only recognise it in terms of what we know today. That means no corporate jargon, acronyms or pseudo-intellectual verbiage.

There are many ways a vision can be framed, but here are two starters to try.

'How might we ...?'

Borrowed from the problem-solving approach 'design thinking', using 'How might we' (HMW) statements is a simple yet powerful way to reframe problems to positively define them as an opportunity (Figure 3.1).

- **How**: suggests that we don't yet have the answer. It allows us to consider multiple avenues for innovation and reinforces that we're still exploring the challenge.
- **Might**: emphasises that there are many different paths we can go down when thinking about solutions. This allows for thinking about the problem from different angles. This 'might' is where innovation becomes part of the process!

How might we .... for .... in order to ....

Figure 3.1 'How might we' statement.

- **We**: immediately brings in the idea of teamwork, rather than a mission gifted by senior executives. Everyone's involved. 'We' should all work collaboratively to come up with a joint understanding of the problem and put our heads together to come up with a joint solution.

An example of this might be:

> *How might we create an engaging and creative workspace for our in-country team and client partners in order to attain the number 1 market position?*

The useful thing about framing the vision as a **question** rather than a statement is that questions hijack our brain; we can't help but try and answer them. A question will engage everyone and make them feel as though they can contribute.

'Together, let's ...'

Another template we can use is 'Together, let's', developed by Kursty. It's more of a statement, but the elements help to frame the opportunity as a collective call to action and the 'why do this?' in an engaging and meaningful way (Figure 3.2).

An example of this might be:

> *Together let's shape a creative and inspiring environment that stimulates and enables creativity by providing spaces that are inspiring, collaborative, social and flexible to our needs so that we can invent the future of [product/industry].*

It's not about getting the vision 'right' at this stage, but more about capturing the essence and intention – it'll evolve over time. What's important is to get people really excited and aligned around the

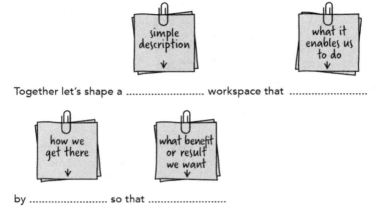

Together let's shape a .... workspace that ....

by .... so that ....

Figure 3.2 'Together, let's' statement.

purpose of our new workspace and its role in supporting the organisation's goals.

WHAT ARE OUR OBJECTIVES?

To show how the vision fits with our objectives, we'll use the first vision statement example as a demo.

Our vision needs to be supported by essential objectives – as in, the things that will need to be achieved and that will take priority when decisions are being made and budgets are being allocated. When we begin to explore the potential drivers behind what our leaders would like our new workspace to achieve, we often see different perspectives and competing priorities begin to play out.

There's no science behind the number of objectives we'll define (three is a good minimum, five a good maximum), other than they need to be **complementary** (too many can create conflicts) and **memorable** (for incredibly busy people).

It's recommended that each objective has a **keyword** and a short **description**. An example of our objectives might be:

- **Growth**: an investment in people – an environment for health, wellbeing, performance and development.
- **Trust**: a workspace that enables people to work when, where and how they choose, and a culture that respects choice.

- **Connection**: a place for people to work openly together, to develop relationships and networks across the organisation.

Our objectives are strengthened when they're backed with qualitative or quantitative metrics that can be captured simply and meaningfully, both during and after the project. For one of the objectives, in this instance growth, these metrics might be as follows:

- Specific facilities for wellbeing designed and included within the workspace – data from the design process.
- Reduction in sickness absence – data from human resources.
- Increase in courses held and completed, certificates obtained and internal promotions gained – data from learning and development.

When this is complete, the vision can sit atop our objectives and metrics blocks (Figure 3.3).

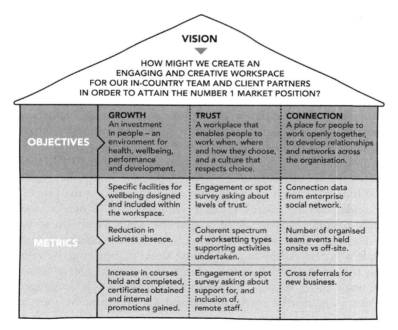

Figure 3.3 Vision house.

As its appearance suggests, it's commonly termed a 'vision house'.

In creating a framework that can develop as the project progresses, with all our key aims and measures in one place, we're setting up some **key performance indicators** (KPIs) for our workspace, as will be covered below.

WHEN DO WE BEGIN THE CHANGE PROCESS?

Developing our vision and objectives is a significant first step in the 'change' process.

It's worth noting that very often change management is seen as a downstream 'plug in', something that someone gets hired to do for us when all the key decisions have been taken. But the *whole project* is one of leading change, and this is the time when we're laying out our map, agreeing where we want to go and setting out on the journey together.

Leading change – as we're doing here, with a new workspace – means three things:

- **Informing** our colleagues what's happening (so they **know** something about it).
- **Engaging** them (so they **feel** positive about the change).
- **Involving** them (so they **do** something beneficial for themselves and to help others).

Activities across each of the above need to be happening concurrently, although we may start by telling colleagues what's happening, why, when and how. Before initiating a programme that weaves a variety of different activities together. We'll cover more on this in Part III.

While we've been engaging with colleagues during the process of understanding, there'll come a point where we'll need to formally commit, emotionally if not at this stage legally (in terms of contracts such as a lease). That is, to tell our colleagues that while we've been thinking and talking about it, capturing the valuable insight of our colleagues, something *is definitely going to happen*. Sharing a rough version of the proposed timeline as it's envisaged at this stage can be incredibly helpful for everyone. So long as we keep timings approximate and loose enough to give a feel for what's about to happen without over-promising.

There's no right or wrong as to when we 'go public' with the workspace project. We may choose to do this later, and at this stage simply let our colleagues know we're thinking about it and doing some background data gathering. Whenever we decide, we'll need the help of our organisation's communications team, which we look at early in Part II.

There are some important things to consider when we tell colleagues about the project for the first time:

- Changes to workspace can be **emotive**. We need to keep in mind that what we're doing is an opportunity to *genuinely make working life better for our colleagues*. The words we use should reflect this, be expressed in the positive, be optimistic and focus on opportunity.
- We should state **what we can** and be clear on what we don't yet know or can't say with certainty. It's okay to say that we're going to be moving (if we are) but we don't know or can't say where yet. If say nothing, our colleagues will fill in the gaps, or make assumptions and we'll spend energy and time managing rumours. No one expects us to know everything at this stage. Better to set up an open mindset from the beginning to get an honest dialogue going.
- The announcement is a good opportunity to indicate that things are changing by using a different **style** – perhaps some words not normally used (lexicon), and a different graphical approach to the usual organisational memo that gets deleted before being read. (Yes, everyone does it).
- Create a **channel** for dialogue. We're not in the 'no reply' business. The views, emotions and insights of our colleagues are incredibly valuable, and we need to know about them. Discomfort or uncertainty is normal, and not something to be overcome, but understood.

All our project communication from here needs to pass some tests before being released it. It must be:

- **Clear**: incredibly, however clear we think we're being, we can always be clearer.

- **Concise**: we need to say what we need to say, and nothing more. Attention spans are often short. Waffling can make it feel like we're hiding something.
- **Interesting**: we want our colleagues to devour the whole message.
- **Balanced**: some news will be good, some not so good – we mustn't try and dress the bad up in false frills.
- **Genuine**: it needs to sound like a human, talking to humans – not an imagined view of how a 'corporation' would speak.
- **Inclusive**: it needs to speak to everyone, irrespective of their experience or position with the company.
- **Honest**: the whole truth, and nothing but the truth – better to say 'we don't know' than nothing at all, or worse still, making something up in an attempt to appease.
- **Multichannel**: it's not just about email. People work in different ways using a range of tools, so we'll need to make sure we reflect how they communicate.
- **Continuous:** while being very careful not to dial up the volume on already noisy email and messaging streams, we can't assume that just because we've said something once, through one specific channel, that the message will have been received and understood.

That's quite a lot of tests. As the energy on the project ramps up, it's easy to lose sight of them, but they'll serve us well as we progress, so it's important to plan a programme of communications ahead of diving in.

DO WE NEED TO DEVELOP A WORKSPACE PLAYBOOK?

Our project may involve the only workspace our organisation has, in which case the development of our vision, requirements and design will be a one-off, self-contained exercise.

However, we may either have – or intend to have – more workspace in other locations. In this regard, we may wish to ensure some commonality of approach. Another early step in the change process, therefore, may be the development of a workspace 'playbook'. This is an outline guide to how a workspace for the organisation should be created, able to be adapted for different locations to reflect local context from cultural norms through to legal requirements.

This is a task often completed by an interior architect as it involves experience of creating workspace and the ability to output plans and visuals. A workspace playbook often includes:

- Overall vision for the organisation's workspace – what it's for and what outcomes are desired.
- How the workspace will support hybrid working (if applicable).
- Design principles.
- Approach to general layout, including work, social and learning space.
- Typical worksettings to be deployed (the 'kit of parts').
- Specific requirements relating to matters such as wellbeing, inclusion, technology, audio visual, branding and security.
- Space requirements – potentially a calculator or formula.
- Special requirements for particular functions of the organisation (such as labs, workshops or software development areas).

These items are all covered in Parts I and II of the book.

A playbook can be developed at any time, including:

- Before the project begins, to clarify intent and set clear goals and guidelines. We may seek to engage an interior architect specifically for the task.
- During the project, as the requirements and design develop, using the interior architect selected for our project.
- After the project is complete, considering lessons learned, again using our interior architect.

There's no right or wrong approach related to the development of a playbook. If we do decide to develop one, there are two practicalities to bear in mind:

- During its creation, be prepared to **challenge** what needs to be included. Playbooks can become overly complex in trying to cover everything – as we'll address during the book, workspace needs to remain simple and intuitive to maximise colleague appeal and use.

- In its use, always maintain flexibility and to **adapt** it with time and experience. Some things will work, and others won't. It should be a living, changing resource.

HOW MUCH SPACE WILL WE NEED?

Workspace calculation is the challenge of matching (often highly variable) demand with (comparatively static) supply.

It's a calculation we often need to make early in our project, before our professional team is assembled. Particularly where it's needed to inform feasibility, a budget calculation or a market search. Or, as is often the case, all three. That is, to get the project off the ground at all. It may have been covered in our workspace playbook if this is something we've created.

For those locations where roles necessitate presence, or a full attendance mandate is in place, the workspace calculation may remain relatively easy. We'll simply need to factor in an idea of potential growth. But where there's hybrid working based on choice and attendance is variable, the challenge will be to provide enough space to meet peak demand but not so much that at other times the workspace looks and feels (or is) empty.

For all workspace attendance approaches, while we may have past and present data and an idea of trends, we're always taking an informed guess about the future. We'll likely want our workspace to support new behaviours, patterns and ways of working that may not reflect what's happening today.

Our overall requirement will need to consider:

- **General workspace**: desks, tables and benches for individuals and teams, storage and circulation space.
- **Informal meeting spaces**: spaces for impromptu interaction or meetings that don't require walls and a door, in particular those for small gatherings (up to 4–6 people – noting that these numbers are indicative; our understanding of colleague

behaviour and stated needs will help to inform the size of spaces needed).

- **Virtual meeting spaces**: small, enclosed rooms for 1–3 people, specifically for interacting with colleagues not in the same physical space.
- **Closed meeting rooms**: a range of different sized rooms to accommodate client or visitor-facing meetings, certain types of training, project or confidential work. Specifying the number and size can feel like something of a dark art, given we're attempting to understand capacity and actual attendance, but we can look to our early information gathering, apply some rules of thumb and build in flexibility to help.
- **Amenities**: cafe, gym and wellbeing spaces, to name a few.
- **Special areas**: including labs, staging areas, customer areas, client lounges and the like. Increasingly common special areas are reconfigurable meeting spaces, which are typically formed by furniture elements in open workspaces.

The calculation can be as complex as we choose to make it, since there is a wide range of potential variables. Note that adding more variables doesn't necessarily ensure a better outcome – it may, in fact, confuse the picture.

TRUE STORY

Working on a project in a major European city, the space requirement for around 200 people was determined by the number of window bays for each grade of seniority. Initially at a junior level the offices were shared, and then at a more senior level individually assigned. In our market search, we found what we thought was the perfect workspace and then calculated how many window bays were needed on a spreadsheet, using the number of people at each grade. Overall, we were a window bay short. No-one was prepared to concede a window bay. And so, the search continued …

We have three choices in how we determine our initial space requirement:

1   Do it ourselves, with the intention that the interior architect appointed for our project will check and validate it at a later stage as part of their assignment (their role is described early in Part II). If we do this, it's highly recommended that it's validated by a professional (options 2 and 3) before any formal commitment is made to leasing or buying workspace.
2   Secure the services of a suitably skilled space planner or interior architect for this assignment alone, or as part of the development of a playbook (mentioned earlier).
3   Tender early for the services of an interior architect who will be involved for the whole project. This is described in Part II.

There are two approaches we can use to determine our space requirement:

*   **Demand-led**: the most common approach to date, which estimates the amount of space we think we'll need based on who we think will use it and what they'll need to do. We're creating *input* to a calculation by identifying everything to be included.
*   **Supply-led**: a relatively rare approach until the pandemic – which starts with an amount of space we think we'll have (or can afford) and working back from there who can use it and what might be done in it. This method generates an *output*, as in, the allowance.

The optimum process will often involve a combination of the two and can entail a far more detailed build-up of the requirement that results in a **space budget**, which is a detailed spreadsheet listing all the space components and worksettings covered in Part II, together with quantities and an estimate of space required for each and circulation spaces between. This gives us a rolled-up total space requirement. Space budgets can be useful, as they go beyond simply estimating the space required, giving a clear picture of the proportions of different types of space (and how our future plans compare with the old). However, this level of detail is not necessarily required at this stage of our project.

Demand-led method

To generate a space requirement, there are several steps:

1   Multiply the **attendee number** by the prevailing market-level amount of **space per person** – we can assume that needs varying by role or function will even themselves out overall. A useful, modern-day rate would be 10–12 sq m (108 – 130 sq ft). This will vary by country and location.
2   Add a percentage to this total space requirement for **amenities** and special areas – this can be around 10-15% depending on how social the space is intended to be or whether we'll have a lot of visitors.
3   Add a weighting to this total for the **type** of workspace we're creating. For example, a city centre legal firm with client suite may require more space per head than an out-of-town customer contact centre. We might use a multiple of 1.2 for the professional services workspace, while for the customer contact space we might use 0.8.
4   Take our final figure and **round it down**, accounting for the act that we'll select a building with efficient architecture and apply intelligent workspace design.

Our calculation might look something like this for a professional services workspace with client lounge, cafe, client-facing meeting suite and wellbeing facilities. We'll use square metres for the purpose of this example (Figure 3.4).

Other considerations can then be applied to help refine our approximation, usually downwards:

*   **History** of workspace attendance: our organisation may have a 'leaning' towards high or low attendance for various reasons (culture, management, process).
*   **Time elapsed** since the last major workspace renovation or move, which will likely reflect our present stage of workspace maturity and hence the size of the leap we may need to make from where we're at today to a modern, energised workspace.
*   **Location** and transport matters: connectivity matters given our heightened sensitivity to the time spent commuting,

including the possibility that some people moved out of cities and suburbs during the pandemic, and our organisation may have recruited new people in more distant locations, which will impact numbers we need to accommodate.

- The **shape** of the space. We'll likely need less space than our derived target if the space is 'efficiently' arranged (simple shapes, such as squares and rectangles, and with lots of usable space) and filled with daylight, but more if it's inefficient (unusable due to structural or circulation features, or not easily configured), light-starved space.

- Pure and simple **gut feel**. There's little science involved in our calculation given there are so many elements that are subject to judgment. A healthy and prudent 'rounding down' is more advisable that a rounding up. Every square metre or foot of space we can liberate has a cost and commitment (and hence saving opportunity) attached.

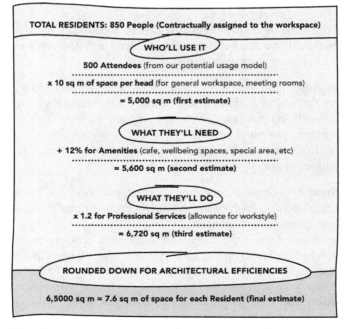

Figure 3.4 Space requirements calculation.

Supply-led methods

If estimating space demand is working forwards, then supply-led methods are working backwards. The starting point is based on two main needs – affordability and function – and we then think about how best to get the most value from it.

Very often location is a major consideration here, in the same way we might personally choose a place to live. For example, for a given cost, do we choose:

- **Quality**: a tiny flat or apartment in a cool, vibrant and connected neighbourhood; or
- **Quantity**: a multi-bedroom detached house in a sleepy backwater?

The same goes for functionality. For example, if the focus of the workspace is client engagement, location and access may dictate the options to be considered. If it's a 'back office', processing and administering, access to labour may be a higher priority.

'Gut feel' plays a far more prominent role here. In the previous example used for the demand-led calculation, we may decide to accept high rental costs on 2,500 sq m (26,900 sq ft) in a talent-rich area and work out how we'll design and use the workspace from there. In a post-pandemic world of uncertainty, it's by no means wrong to plan this way. We may even discover once we've moved in that we didn't need that extra 1,500 sq m (16,145 sq ft) after all.

Split requirements

It's becoming increasingly common post-pandemic for workspace to be split between leased, dedicated space to account for the bulk of expected regular use, and several other types of non-dedicated space to account for variations in demand. Much of course depends on location and the offering in the vicinity of any dedicated space. The alternatives are covered in the next chapter.

Essentially, however, a key question to ask at this stage is – *do we need to provide all our own workspace?*

Thinking about organisational growth

Most organisations anticipate growing. Which means more people. This is likely to be either organic growth, or the result of a merger or acquisition. Each presents its own challenges:

- **Merger** or **acquisition**: there will usually be a people and property rationalisation process to remove costs from duplication. Sometimes this is immediate, sometimes after a period of assessment. We'll likely know it's coming (not always guaranteed, however, if we've not been invited into the 'inner circle') and will be able to plan for it.
- **Organic growth**: a notoriously difficult challenge for those within and those outside the organisation to find out by how many people and when, particularly considering the number of possible factors likely to influence the degree. However, there's usually at least some form of estimate or projection available.

Given the time lag from idea to completion of our workspace, a tendency to build in assumptions of growth to the space requirements often arises.

However, there are natural downward pressures on space requirements, too:

- Changes in **working culture** resulting in greater day to day flexibility – the shift to hybrid being the most significant of these.
- Greater acceptance of space and **worksetting sharing**, particularly with variable patterns of attendance.
- Advancement of **workspace technology** facilitating further flexibility.

We need to be careful, therefore, not to simply add (say) 10% to our space requirements for future growth that may or may not occur. We must also be confident that, apart from workspace where people are allocated a specific worksetting, most workspace **can absorb more usage** without our needing to increase the amount of floorspace, subject to statutory limits described below.

Statutory limits

Fortunately, we can't just squeeze ever-increasing numbers of people into a workspace when demand exceeds the seats available.

There are what are termed 'statutory provisions', which are limits governed by laws or regulations that in most countries relate to fire evacuation, fresh air supply, heating and cooling, and toilet provision. These limits protect the health, safety and wellbeing of individuals.

The methods of calculating each provision will need the help of a technical specialist. This is best undertaken during the due diligence phase of evaluating our shortlist of building options covered in Part II, as they relate to the building itself and not so much what we might do with our design. However, we can if needed augment some of the features where the building provision isn't adequate for our needs, such as adding toilets in our floorspace.

Most workspaces don't reach their statutory limits, but 'back office' and contact centre locations can often get close. For most workspaces with hybrid working, however, it's become a more complex consideration as we're generally working with peak attendance to calculate capacity rather than a regular number of people expected in the workspace daily. Which means at this stage, we need a working estimate, probably based on our existing workspace, and we'll also need to know how many people are present each day ongoing. If we think we might be approaching the statutory limit, we'll also need an alert mechanism and potentially a plan for managing the potential scenario where the limit may be exceeded.

DO WE NEED OUR *OWN* WORKSPACE?

We now have a more aligned idea of what we want from our workspace, the priorities or areas that it needs to deliver upon and an idea of the amount of space we'll need. The next question is: do we need our own workspace, or should we share space – all or in part?

There are many workspaces available that provide space for a variety of size of groups of people, either in a dedicated area for a given period, or on a pay-as-you-go basis. This is often termed 'flexi-space'.

The approach has several advantages:

- Space is available only when it's needed, that won't be wasted when it's not.
- Shorter commitment should things change (which they will).
- No need to create space ourselves – an expert does it for us and does it well (so we can put this book down now).
- Access to a variety of shared amenities that wouldn't be economical in a small, dedicated workspace.
- Support for a more dispersed workforce, with small centres in a variety of locations.

It also has several disadvantages:

- No (or little) ability to personalise or brand the space.
- Higher day-to-day cost (flexibility comes at a price).
- It's not always possible to secure the shared amenities (e.g. meeting rooms) when needed.
- Lack of security of tenure, in that we may be asked to move or leave – flexibility can work both ways.
- Risks to the security of the organisation from sharing workspace – to its property, people and information (analogue and digital).

We're assuming we've weighed it up and decided, on balance, that we need (or perhaps at this stage, that we'd *like*) our own workspace.

WHAT ALTERNATIVES ARE THERE TO US HAVING A WORKSPACE?

There are three alternatives to us having a workspace, any (or a combination) of which might be viable depending on circumstances. Together with workspaces dedicated to organisations they form what's become known as the workspace 'ecosystem', which means that instead of being restricted to just one place to work, we have the option of working in each of them as needed.

1   **Home**: kitting out an employee to work from their own home is considerably easier and cheaper than creating a

workspace – assuming the employee has the space and willingness to do so. There are several considerations in developing a home-working approach:

a. What kit to provide, and how it's maintained and returned
b. What to expense (connectivity, energy usage etc)
c. Security of data and other materials
d. Standards for home broadband
e. Insurance
f. Health and safety
g. Employment contract.

2 **Urban amenities**: towns and cities increasingly offer workspaces in places including cafes, hotels, libraries and retail outlets. These may range from simply enabling work to take place there (e.g. providing Wi-Fi), to dedicated spaces designed for work. They offer opportunities for a change of environment and the company of other people, yet their low cost is often offset by distractions and inconveniences (e.g. noise or tables not suited to long stretches of work). This is a genre that is likely to expand in type and quantity in the near future, as non-workspaces seek to diversify in the wake of reduced post-pandemic urban footfall.

3 **Coworking spaces**: these fully built-for-purpose working environments often require a monthly membership subscription or daily fee. Coworking spaces come with the added benefit of a (mostly) like-minded community, and often feature curated activities and events designed to bring members together socially and professionally. Networks of coworking spaces have the added advantage of offering additional spaces to choose from, which can be useful when travelling or arranging to meet colleagues from out of the area.

It should be noted that the distinction between flexi-spaces and coworking spaces is rarely clear-cut. Flexi-spaces often have less formal, drop-in membership areas, and coworking spaces often have areas dedicated to particular groups or organisations.

Each of the above may be a suitable place for task work, but rarely in the company of people from our own organisation. Our goal with this book is the creation of spaces for task and exploratory work with colleagues from, and clients of, our own organisation.

That said, this book is equally viable as a guide to creating fantastic coworking spaces.

DO WE FOCUS ON COST OR VALUE?

It's pretty much inevitable that the age-old debate about cost (the money that leaves) and value (the benefit that arrives) is going to arise when it comes to figuring out how or where to invest in space.

People are generally more comfortable with talking about cost because it's:

- **Visible** and **tangible** – we're going to have to order and pay for stuff.
- **Immediate** –it's likely the business won't commit until there's a clear idea of it.
- Easy to **identify** and **measure** – everyone understands it, it's connected to the 'bottom line'.
- Enables simple trade-offs – it's easy to **choose** one thing over another given a fixed budget.

Value is much trickier:

- It can take **time** to emerge and become visible, so we're not always aware of it at the time decisions need to be made.
- We don't have a common **measure** – in many instances, even any kind of measure at all – and so can't make comparisons or trade-offs.
- It's usually **unevenly** distributed through the organisation, and through time.

Take the case of whether to design an appropriate cafe space and employ a barista. It's easy to estimate the capital cost of the counters, machinery etc and the operating cost of employing someone suitably skilled to run it. But it's more difficult to capture and understand the value of the conversations that take place and connections that are made as colleagues are drawn into the space due to the excellent products and service.

Very often value-based decisions must be taken on trust and extrapolated from insights gleaned from our research. Similarly, new measures may need to be devised to qualify or quantify the value (as discussed at the beginning of this chapter). What's important, however, is the recognition that decisions are always a matter of cost/value balance. Beware an over-focus on cost at every turn; it can ultimately detract from delivering value.

TRUE STORY

A public sector organisation had committed to move to agile working, with an accompanying workspace overhaul. External advisers undertook the analytics, vision and objective setting, developed design principles and conducted the culture change workshops. The organisation's leadership was enthused and ready. A new building that would have been perfect for their teams was identified, but after delays in setting out the business case, it was snapped up by another tenant. Three years later, the advisers heard the authority were still trying to perfect the business case to satisfy their internal processes. In the meantime, the costs of the move had risen, and frustration had set in. There comes a point when commitment needs to be made based on the best available information.

Adding a little more difficulty to our cost/value consideration, we should also be aware that we'll need a **'fast lane'** and a **'slow lane'** in our workspace. Sometimes colleagues will be in a hurry – things to do, places to be. They'll want a push-button, no-delay solution. Task work will be calling.

At other times, we'll need to encourage colleagues to dwell, to talk and spend time together, as that's how connections are made, and trust is built. This is where exploratory work can begin. So, when we consider cost and value, we can't just consider our choices in terms of productive 'task work' outcomes.

Using this lens to look at our workspace, we can consider how to add real value to the experience for our colleagues and the organisation.

WHAT SHOULD WE SPEND OUR MONEY ON?

All workspace projects will face spending choices, however frugal (or not) the approach. The challenge will be to spend money on the right things. There are some guiding principles:

- **Re-use**: anything working, in good condition and/or tells a story of who we are/where we've come from. As covered earlier, we should by now have an accurate inventory. This should be balanced against the intent of the new workspace, however: older style, larger desks for example may negatively impact the overall space efficiency or quality of colleague interactions through proximity.
- Seek **substitutions**: but avoid cost reduction for its own sake. There's usually a cheaper version out there, but we need to be mindful of quality, origins and hidden costs (see below).
- Consider **whole life** costs, including warranties, maintenance and service. What may appear to be a more expensive option may turn out to be lower cost over time. Sometimes choices of this nature reveal a flaw in the process of capital budgeting, in that the focus is on what's spent today.
- **Design better**: it's easy in a workspace project to spend a king's ransom without taking a breath. But great outcomes more often result from great design. That is, considered solutions to problems as opposed to ostentatious materials or 'big names'. While design (and most professional) fees are often questioned because they don't appear to relate to anything immediately tangible, a little more time and money spent on design can yield a lower spend overall and a far better outcome. For example, a clever use of space can reduce footprint and therefore reduce running costs, or elegant wayfinding elements can make orientation both easy and interesting.

TRUE STORY

The office of an organisation known for its 'respectfully rebellious' innovation team was paradoxically dark and cluttered, a stark contrast to their dynamic mantras like 'fail fast, fail forward'. Despite championing creativity, daylight was blocked by ever-drawn blinds for 'confidentiality', and the corners were cluttered with untouched whiteboards and a bizarre collection of makeshift rubbish bins. A collective brainstorm led by one of the authors inspired a simple yet transformative night operation. Desk numbers were halved, allowing confidential areas to be created and letting sunlight flood in by day. The excessive and under-questioned bins were shown the exit. This low-cost, high-impact revamp unlocked a brighter, more energetic space that truly reflected the team's innovative spirit. Sometimes, innovation isn't just about what you add, but also what you remove—and that might just include taking out the trash in more ways than one.

It's as useful to look at what's worth spending money on as what isn't. We should aim to spend money to benefit the following categories, as these are the most likely creators of value and the tests we should apply to what we create:

- **Performance**: enabling colleagues to work effectively, whether alone or together (e.g. quality chairs, technology, acoustics).
- **Wellbeing**: worksettings and amenities to make our work and lives better, through comfort, ease of use and functionality (e.g. plants, food, quiet spaces).
- **Connection**: worksettings and amenities that help create and develop relationships, enabling conversation and encouraging people to dwell – very much in our slow lane (e.g. space for learning or relaxing with others).
- **Endurance**: areas of high traffic and objects of frequent use that need to be robust in order to stand the test of time (e.g. circulation spaces, support amenities).
- **Impact**: delivering 'wow' to colleagues, customers and visitors, emphasising the brand and values of the organisation.

(e.g. entrances, social and leisure amenities, formal meeting or demonstration spaces – potentially even the washrooms!).

Equally, we should avoid spending money where it may simply result in cost that's difficult to justify or adds no apparent value. In particular, where it serves:

- **Hierarchy**: most workspaces in the post-pandemic era have embodied greater levels of flexibility and sharing, given variable attendance and the desire to get 'more from less'. Gone are the days where the corner office comes as standard for executives.
- **Habit**: the past has never been so useless in determining the future. Now is the time to challenge previous assumptions. That's not to say that sometimes these assumptions may be proven to be valuable.
- **Mimicry**: as mentioned earlier, what's good for another organisation is probably not good for us. We're not them. Seeing the workspace of other organisations is useful for ideas, but copying it isn't helpful. Plus, it'll be obvious and we'll just look a little desperate.
- **Complexity**: the specification of some workspaces can get out of hand. Working patterns and needs are often very simple and predictable. As a rule, if a feature or worksetting needs any form of explanation as how to use it or what to do in it, it's too complex.
- **Whim**: we should take care with the value of 'Impact'. If overdone, it can sometimes spill over into an indulgent flight of fancy, the regret over which will endure.

Let's talk about **form** and **function**.

Since Roman times it's been well established that something must work (function) before it looks beautiful (form). However, in good design function can be its form – it's beautiful *because* it does what it needs to do. While we strive for functional workspace, we do need to satisfy our need for beauty as well, which can be as much in the way something adjusts, what it communicates about us and our organisation as the elegance of its simplicity. Justification for our design should be rooted in the needs, both functional and emotional, of our colleagues and the organisation, not the indulgent expression of the most senior or loudest person in the room.

HOW WILL WE MEASURE SUCCESS?

At this stage of the project, it's a good time to consider the measures we can use to assess if we're being – and when complete, have been – successful.

These key performance indicators (KPIs) can be derived from several sources:

- Our **vision** and **objectives**.
- An alternative measurement **framework**. Kursty has previously published a model with five 'Es' of a fantastic workplace and Neil has created a framework with six 'Es', both built on Frank Duffy's original three 'Es': efficiency, effectiveness and expression (ideas beginning with E evidently being very popular!). These can be found in the resources listed at the end of the book.
- A **bespoke** set of measurements devised specifically for the project, and neither of the above.

It's highly recommended that the first of these is used, even if existing or newly created frameworks input to the formulation of the vision and objectives. Whichever is used, it's become apparent since the pandemic that KPIs need to consider two factors:

- The **performance** of the workspace itself. These KPIs are often established workplace industry measures, such as utilisation (how many people are there and when) and satisfaction (point-in-time sentiment surveys); and
- The **contribution** it's making to the organisation to justify the investment in creating it. These are business-related measures that the workplace industry hasn't to date been especially keen or equipped to capture. We'll therefore need to identify and work closely with colleagues who can obtain this data.

They're always better agreed at the outset so that 'before' and 'after' measures can be taken. Which sounds easier than it often is because the project itself often contributes to our understanding of what we're trying to achieve and evolves our vision and objectives as we progress. So, we shouldn't get too fixated on a perfect before/after alignment.

CAN WE START NOW?

At this stage, we have a good grounding in why we're doing this, how we're going to do it and what we need to do. We've got a clear vision and objectives, and a means of assessing how we're doing. We now need to get on with it.

Some of what we'll cover in the next section will build on what we've already established, some will be new. We're about to get some help from outside the organisation, get more of our colleagues involved inside, and start the design process.

Which means – as design is always exciting – if we've raced through some of this part of the book in a bid to get started, we need to go back and make sure the building blocks are in place. The danger if they're not, as we've already called out, is the increased risk of cost, delay and a degree of failure. We say degree because failure with regard a new workspace is rarely absolute. But it'll remind us it's there every day. And we're all about doing this properly and enjoying it.

THINGS TO LOOK OUT FOR

Here are some of the things to look out for in this area, and to challenge or avoid where possible:

- **'We want the world's best workspace'**: the authors have heard this aim expressed many times, particularly by CEOs. While a desire to be 'the best' is admirable, creating the very best is quite an ask, and somewhat vague. There are no objective measures of such, and as a result, the holder of the accolade at any point in time is unknown. Such a lofty aim will also be impacted by factors such as the base building we're working with, and the time and money available. We can be ambitious – but need to keep it realistic and relevant, too.

- **'Kitchen sinking'**: the tendency to include almost every idea and buzzword imaginable in the vision and objectives. Sometimes as a failsafe, sometimes due to the lack of time available (or inclination) to hone and develop the content; or possibly because it just seems like the right thing to do. The more we include, the less we can focus on each, the less we'll remember and the less meaning any measurement of success will be. Less, however, really is more.
- **Coworking – our way?** its undeniable that coworking has changed our view of what makes a fantastic workspace. Whether through their relaxed aesthetic, dog-friendly welcome, 'common room' vibe or amenities (such as free beer) that aren't found in typical corporate workspace, organisations have attempted to mimic many aspects within their own space and used the term 'coworking' to describe particular areas of the workspace. But care is needed – coworking is much less about space and more about **community**. The space itself happens to be the gravitational hub for people from disparate backgrounds and industries to interact. It's only coworking if its community focussed and involves people from inside and outside the organisation. Otherwise, it's simply workspace …

PART II

HOW DO WE MAKE OUR WORKSPACE REAL?

4

SET-UP
HOW WILL WE RUN THE PROJECT?

As our project ramps us, we can't do all this on our own. We're going to need the right people with us from within and outside the organisation – and to ensure they all work together effectively.

WHO WILL NEED TO BE INVOLVED?

No matter how big our project – in terms of space size, budget or ambition – we'll need some help. The project will impact everyone in the organisation who comes to the workspace, so at the very least they need to be kept in the loop around progress. Better than that, if we consider who to involve and at what stage in the project will lay the path for a smoother journey, when we hit the inevitable bump in the road, we can call on various people to help keep things on track.

We'll need people to help us from inside and outside the organisation. The people inside the organisation will be needed to help make decisions, communicate and gather information, solve specialist problems and help us find and onboard the people from

DOI: 10.4324/9781003442684-6

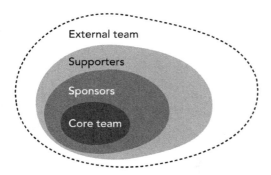

Figure 4.1 Project support environment.

outside. External people will provide specialist skills or resources we don't have internally.

Overall, our support environment looks as shown in Figure 4.1.

WHAT INTERNAL HELP WILL WE NEED?

These roles are the first three layers of our support environment.

Core team

Whichever way a team is set up, someone's got to be on point, ultimately responsible, and for whom the project will be the 'day job' until it's finished. As you're reading this book, it's assumed it's you.

Around the internal project manager will need to be a core team, an inner circle of around 4-8 people (or as few as two if it's a small transformation). These people need to have both:

- **Commitment**: they care enough about the positive impact that the working environment can have on the effectiveness of their colleagues and the organisation that they're prepared to communicate regularly and implement consistently – even if the project happens to be 'side-of-the-desk'.

- **Time**: they need to have enough scope in their day/week to do what's needed, rather than the project responsibility being added to an already unmanageable pile. Some may need to bring in their own temporary help either for the project or to back-fill their roles for the time required.

They're usually drawn from the typical functions of an organisation, shown below, but may also be from none of them – they could be specialist project managers, process experts, fast-track management trainees – the scope is wide.

Sponsors

A small group of senior stakeholders who will make and sign-off decisions, open doors and influence leadership as needed. The decision-making process and role of the Steering Group is outlined in the next section.

Supporters

Outside of the core team, other people within the organisation will need to be called upon at various stages in the project. They'll each bring different perspectives and experience, and in some cases will be an essential pair of hands to make things happen.

It's worth identifying and talking to the functions shown below to establish who's best to be involved, and whether they'll be in the core team or simply our 'go-to' person. A rough list, in order of priority might be:

- **Human resources** (HR): It's become increasingly common for HR to have a key role in creating a new workspace, sometimes even lead it, especially if our workspace project is linked to an organisational transformation. If there's a relocation involved, there may be contractual issues. HR may also have a designated 'change' role. It's also likely that a member of the HR team will be able to advise on **equality, diversity and inclusivity** (ED&I). Suffice to say, HR's potential contribution needs to be scoped with them at the outset.

- **Information technology** (IT): most workspace projects include a huge slice of 'tech' – infrastructure, hardware and applications (apps). In addition, other projects and business-as-usual want a slice of the IT team, too, so early engagement and the setting out of their likely commitment is advisable.

- **Finance**: the availability of money and a process for setting up multiple new suppliers, some of whom may require terms that deviate from our standard ones is essential, so the accountants must be primed early. There will also likely be a member of the Finance team nominated to act as the internal cost manager, able to navigate the organisation's financial systems and meet its internal reporting and approval requirements.

- **Procurement**: as there'll be a lot to buy, much of which will likely require tendering, so putting a procurement plan in place will be vital. A fast-moving workspace project can't afford to get bogged down in process. Some product or service selection decisions may also need a 'fast track' as there may not be time to formally tender everything to a minimum of three suppliers.

- **Legal**: contracts will be needed for professional services, construction works, IT and furniture, as well as possibly reviewing and negotiating lease details. Depending on the scale of the project and the construction route we take, there may be multiple complex contracts that require understanding and executing.

- **Communications**: there'll be a 'change' workstream which deals with the whole journey from understanding needs through to defining and delivering the new workspace and ways of working. At times throughout the project, there will be lots of content creation and distribution needed. A comms team member may need to be partially or wholly seconded to the project. If moving location, there's also the complexity associated with the change of address, often involving the **company secretary** or similar function along with HR if employment contracts need changing, too.

- **Facilities management** (FM): the people who'll be running the space must be involved in creating it. That may sound obvious, but it's been a justifiable frustration of the FM industry for many years that involvement is often late, and that on completion they're handed something that doesn't work, either wholly or in part. IT support teams have often had a similar complaint.

- **Sustainability**: depending on the size of the organisation, such are the expected commitments to **environment, social and governance** (ESG) that a dedicated role may exist for setting and managing the organisation's sustainability priorities.
- **Knowledge management**: depending on where knowledge resides within the organisation, there may be a need for scanning, storing or cataloguing information.

A role not to overlook – which is all too often overlooked – is **administration**. It doesn't fit any of the departmental buckets, but every workspace project will demand heaps of it. It's worth bringing someone with super organisational skills into the team as early as possible, for tasks such as file and record keeping, contract logging, meeting and event arranging, meeting minuting and database management. Or the detail may well consume us at some point.

We'll now have an internal project team to get started with.

HOW WILL THE PROJECT BE GOVERNED?

We may have been given the job of running the project, but unfortunately, we won't be the ones making all the decisions. Albeit on occasions being the only one deciding isn't a good place to be, and we'd rather the responsibility be shared. And not just for the colour of the cushion covers.

So, it helps to establish – early on – roles, responsibilities and a process for making (and sticking to) decisions.

Governance of this nature comes in the form of a steering group or committee – as we'll call it, a **SteerCo** It usually comprises core interests – as a minimum, finance, HR/people, IT and general management. Note that these aren't necessarily 'roles', but there should be representation across these areas. Also note that, if the CEO or managing director of the organisation is within the SteerCo, it usually means that all decisions will be taken by them.

If they're not involved, then they need to give the SteerCo the authority to make decisions on their behalf, with a commitment to respect and stand by them. Even if it's discovered too late that the CEO doesn't like yellow cushions.

It's a well-worn adage that 'a camel is a horse created by a committee'. So just declaring a SteerCo doesn't guarantee the right decisions, or that they will be made on time. We need a rigorous process, including:

- A commitment on the part of each member to attend every SteerCo meeting, holidays and emergencies excepted.
- Prioritised calendar invites (monthly is a good rhythm).
- A 'standing' agenda (structured with the same topics every session).
- A content creator – someone who collates all relevant information in the form of a slide deck, usually – that's likely to be us.
- A prompt for all key decisions that need to be made.
- A method of taking and agreeing minutes and decisions.
- A meeting chairperson – preferably not us, for independence from the day-to-day running of the project.

When it comes to workspace decisions, objectivity can sometimes be hard to achieve. SteerCo members will arrive with their own personal views and preferences on the way they (and sometimes their team) like to work. We'll have a diplomatic task with the SteerCo to ensure decisions are taken in the best overall interests of the organisation, so we'll need to heavily rely on data gathered, insights gleaned and vision alignment to help keep things on track.

There's also a useful approach we can use to help when we know there are tough decisions to be made. There's a Japanese expression for it – *'nemawashi'* – which literally means 'going around the roots'. This involves talking to each member of the SteerCo *before* a tricky subject is raised to secure support, so there are no surprises during the SteerCo meeting, and the session merely becomes a rubber-stamp for the decision. During these pre-SteerCo conversations, we may gain useful insight or advice that will better shape the request. This may take some time on our part, but it's time very well spent.

WHAT OUTSIDE HELP WILL WE NEED?

The external help we secure will depend on the construction route we take. This can be tricky, as we may not know what's possible or have decided until we at least have our Project Manager on board to help advise us.

Essentially the distinctions are to do with whether the roles needed are part of the construction supply chain, or independent of it. There's no objective right or wrong in terms of the decision needed, only a consideration of what's right for us.

The professional services all get performed somewhere, so it's worth our while understanding what they do. At this stage we'll set out the roles, and thereafter show how they might be secured dependent upon the construction decision.

There are two 'tiers' of services we'll need to bring on board. The main 'tier 1' services, as in those who'll be involved for most of the project with multiple service responsibilities, are:

- **Project manager** (PM): the core team are managing the project internally, the PM in this case is the 'external' project manager. They'll look after and manage the other consultants and construction contractor, and make sure the job gets done on time, on budget and to the expected level of quality. It's worth bringing them on first to assist with the selection of the other consultants, and to advise on the construction procurement options.
- **Cost consultant** (CC): they'll manage the budget – principally all the costs committed to externally, and only those that are 'client direct' or internal recharges if they're told about them – and be able to estimate costs and tell us if something is incorrectly priced. For small workspace projects the PM and CC may be one and the same person or firm.
- **Workplace strategist**: helps to define what's needed through a discovery process usually comprising a series of interviews and workshops, a survey and data collection such as present workspace utilisation (how many people attend, when and where). It may also include recommending the amount and type of space needed. Their report then informs the design

process. Sometimes they stay for the duration of the project as guardians of the vision and objectives, at other times their work is complete after the strategy report is accepted. They can be independent, or part of the external project team such as the interior architect.

- **Interior architect** (IA): sometimes referred to as an interior designer or workspace designer, are often used interchangeably. While interior architects tend to focus more on the functionality of spaces within buildings, interior designers historically would focus more on aesthetics. Any reputable workplace designers will take both into account. They produce the design of the physical workspace, including what it comprises and how the space is arranged, and specify items such as colours, materials, finishes and furniture.

- **Mechanical and electrical designer** (M&E): the less glamorous but just-as-important designer, responsible for designing and specifying systems that govern heating, cooling, fresh air, electrical, water and waste.

- **IT designer**: responsible for IT infrastructure (networks including data and Wi-Fi), desktop equipment and set-up, audio visual (AV) installations, security systems, voice communications and a variety of applications. Some of the IT infrastructure may be specified in-house, and subject to existing local or global supplier agreements, but the designer will draw it all together and document what's needed.

- **Planning consultant**: if the project involves works outside of a building or to an owned building, it may entail dealing with planning permissions, securing approval to works to protected building, highways works, landscaping requirements, local authority obligations, car parking and access.

- **Change manager**: a role that may sometimes be undertaken internally, the Change Manager ensures that the occupants-to-be of the workspace understand it and are ready to explore the opportunities presented by the new workspace to work differently. It's a service often offered by workplace strategy or interior architect firms.

Then there are what we may term 'tier 2' or specialist professional services, that may also be sourced from the supply chain or be independent, including (but not exclusively):

- **Furniture**: the interior architect will usually recommend and detail furniture, but there are also independent consultants around, too. Or we might approach a furniture dealer who'll recommend products they can supply competitively. It's usually best to agree an approach with the interior architect and project manager. Note that furniture manufacturers will rarely supply directly, they prefer a dealer to take on the administration, storage and delivery tasks.
- **Acoustics**: while the interior architect will consider the use of materials to absorb sound and to protect worksettings and work areas from the potential for noise transfer and disturbance, an acoustic specialist can ensure that the environment manages sensitivities to environmental noise in order to be as inclusive as possible across the spectrum of our colleagues.
- **Planting**: the growing awareness of the positive impact of the inclusion of plants and natural materials on productivity and cognitive performance ('biophilia') means that internal planting will undoubtedly feature in our new workspace. A biophilic design consultant can be useful in defining opportunities for the use of natural materials and planting, designing a scheme and obtaining comparative pricing. Alternatively, the interior architect may work up an outline scheme for tendering that can then be developed further once the planting supplier is appointed.
- **Security**: sometimes within the scope of our IT designers, security comprises both hardware (security barriers, readers, CCTV etc) and apps for access and visitor management. Its complexity shouldn't be under-estimated, and so specialist help may be needed.
- **Health and safety**: while there are requirements regarding the health and safety aspects of construction, a specialist may be needed to specify our own arrangements, depending on the nature of our business. The FM team may be able to cover this area so it's best to ask them first.

- **Environment**: we'll have a responsibility to ensure our new workspace supports our organisation's 'green' goals, covering what we do, what we buy and how we set it up to be operated. Most organisations won't have the skills in house, and so will need specialist help from an early stage of the project.
- **Catering**: depending on our choices regarding how much food and drink will be provided, advice may be needed on the facilities required and options on how they might be operated. Most organisations looking at a cafe area of some description usually have the debate over whether to provide a barista service.

There are five important things at this stage to note when procuring professional involvement in the project.

1   On the face of it, this is a lot of professional help. All the firms will have a preferred way of working and solutions they like to see. They know how projects work and what they need to do. But they must work together. Most of all, from the outset, therefore, their activities will need **co-ordinating**. This is a key task of the project manager, with the help of our administrative colleague.

2   What, in market terms, is **independence**, really? It comes in shades, so we'll need to be happy with the level or independence or inter-reliance between suppliers. Even those who are proven to be completely independent of the supply chain will have preferences for certain approaches, products or services, born of experience and peer knowledge-sharing. To an extent, this network is what we're buying.

3   For the tier 1 roles in particular, we'll need to meet the **actual consultants** in each case before the appointment is confirmed. Being sold the dream by the partners and directors is fine, but very often the person who'll be doing the job day-to-day isn't the one we're first presented with. Sometimes we won't even meet them for several weeks until those with whom we initially engaged have the confidence to step away. So, we'll need to insist we do.

4   Professional services can cost 10–15% of the overall work-space **budget**, depending on our construction procurement route. They're intangible – we're buying advice and not 'stuff' – and so their costs can often be a target for those wielding a red pen. Good advice and design can save far more over the life of the project than a minor de-scope of services or choice based on cost. We must therefore always be careful not to allow (or even encourage) compromise at this stage.

5   Finally, a team of specialists requires **chemistry**. We can't specify or buy it. At the outset, it's either there or it isn't. If it's there we can nurture it, if it's not we can try and build it. But there's a golden rule of the authors that decades of experience teach us: if the team balance or energy doesn't feel right, it's probably not and hoping it'll fix itself never works. If this happens, we'll need to change the team, either through swapping out individuals within appointed firms or replacing firms. It's not something to be ignored!

We must now look at the methods of construction to determine which of these services we need to buy separately, and how we might select our shortlist of each for procurement.

WHAT ARE OUR CONSTRUCTION OPTIONS?

There are essentially two construction procurement methods we need to know about at this stage. Naturally, there are firms who offer variants, but the reason we need to be aware of these two methods is that it'll affect how we buy professional services.

By way of terminology, whichever approach is taken, the **general contractor** will be the firm that takes overall responsibility for the build. They'll employ some of the staff in delivering the scheme, but most of the specialist **trades** will be subcontracted under the general contractor's management.

1   **Design and build** (D&B): a 'one stop shop' managed and delivered by one general contractor who completes all the

work. In this approach, often called 'turnkey', the firm sub-contracts services and trades as needed, and the entire project is priced as a 'lump sum'. The design is costed and the build programmed as it develops. We may choose to hire our own an independent project manager to ensure we make the best choice of D&B contractor and that we're being correctly guided throughout, but we'll not need to select further partners.

2 **Traditional**: or 'design–bid–build'. It's called traditional because it's the way it was always done before D&B emerged as a viable alternative. In this approach, we'll need to assemble the full professional team as described above to design independently and cost a scheme that is then tendered to general contractors in full.

Note that some D&B firms adopt a design-led approach and still clearly delineate the three key project stages – strategy, design and delivery.

A summary of the methods, sufficient for our purposes at this stage, is shown in Figure 4.2.

There's no 'right' way to buy construction and the associated professional services. Both come with pros and cons. Clearly, the D&B route means a lot less professional services procurement but with that comes a lot less choice and flexibility, too. Which is why getting our PM on board first is always a good idea; their advice on which route to take given our circumstances and needs can reap huge benefits. That said, it's worth bearing in mind that our PM will have their own preferences.

It's worth mentioning, budget is often the major driver behind the choice of construction procurement route. However, it's fair to say that the 'extra' costs of professional services via the traditional route will be offset by the additional costs a D&B general contractor will apply under conditions of little or no competition.

Part III of the book sets out the construction procurement choice in more detail.

Design & Build

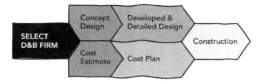

Traditional

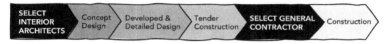

Figure 4.2 Project delivery methods.

HOW DO WE BUY THE SERVICES WE NEED?

Procurement takes time and energy, from research, through process and assessment to appointment. All at the while, we'd rather be getting on with it. Most organisations have a team or person responsible for procurement with their own way of working, and by now we'll have got them involved. But here's a pocket guide to buying professional services for our project.

The steps are:

1   **Research**: for each service we need to buy in, we'll need to identify the ones most likely to be suitable for us. This involves knowledge of the field, diligent research or a mix of both, (our PM can help with this). We'll need 3–4 viable suppliers in each case, all of whom we'd be happy working with, (which will likely be a mix of experience, cost and chemistry).
2   **Request for proposal** (RFP): we ask the suppliers to bid for the work, (also known as 'tender'), or to submit their proposal. 10–14 days can usually be sufficient for them to provide a response. Procurement is a case of 'garbage out, garbage in' – so we must do our part and prepare an excellent RFP. We should also aim to have a standard document we can adjust for each service.

The RFP should contain the following by way of information:

Summary	A summary of everything in the RFP. Crisp, clear, logical and on one page only.
Why	A high-level statement of why the project is going ahead and when.
Context	As much relevant background as possible – who we are, what we do, how we do it, what's changing, our values or principles, and (as we've covered) a diagram showing how the parts of the organisation fit together.
Data	Summaries of all relevant high-level asset and people data.
Aims	What we hope to achieve with the project – reasoned, concise and testable (these become our criteria) – and avoiding pointless waffle.
Practicalities	An outline programme and budget – they may be draft or aspirational subject to the RFP, but something is needed – with a quality expectation. This can be in the form of examples we've found on the shortlisted suppliers' websites, or other examples we've seen that fit our project.
Team	The 'home' team, on a chart, with names and role titles, including any other third parties already contracted. Clearly stating the main points of contact for the tender.
Scope of services	While most professional services firms know what their scope should be, it's best to include it to demonstrate our level of understanding and avoid any potential doubt later. We may need to get this from someone who has done it before.
Process	The supplier will want to know they stand a fair and reasonable chance of winning, so that the investment in bidding is worthwhile. So, the other bidders should be named and the timescale for the process clearly set out.
Criteria	What will be looked for in the RFP response – which shouldn't be absolutely everything or it'll not mean anything. 'Cost' is not wrong; 'chemistry' or 'cultural fit' could be included.
Pricing	A structure for the pricing, if this will help, including our payment terms and anything that may come as a potential surprise.

Other services	Most suppliers offer multiple service lines, not just the ones asked for in the RFP, so a declaration of interest should be requested detailing any other services they may be able to offer with a brief description of what they can do, E.g. Scientific Lab specialism, etc.
References	They must be relevant, so we should state why we need references, what they should show in support of the submission and a structure provided for them (client, size, dates, aims and outcome).
Legal	We'll need to declare any key legal or contractual stipulations of doing business with us as it may affect the price or even the willingness to bid. If we've got a sample contract, it should be included in an appendix.
Structure	Showing the order and number of pages required by subject for the response will make it far easier for evaluation.
Non-compliant bid	Inviting a bid that offers an alternative approach is often welcome – the supplier may see a better way to achieve what's required, and we'd like to know.

The RFP should ask for the following by way of return:

Management summary	Succinct summary of the suppliers' proposal with all salient details including commercial terms.
Supplier's organisation	A summary of the history and function of their organisation, including any data to support their market position and ranking.
Supplier's USP	Why they feel they are the right choice for us and how they're different from their competitors.
Supplier's values	How the values of the supplier's organisation drives their approach and what this will mean for the us in practice.
Supplier's methodology	How they will approach the assignment including the key steps they will take.
Trends	The supplier's understanding of the top three trends within the industry that will have relevance to this assignment – and why they feel they are best placed to understand and interpret each.

(*Continued*)

(Continued)

Understanding of the assignment	What the supplier understands our requirements to be, and any specific clarifications they may need to begin.
Scope of services	The services the supplier will provide within this assignment. Identify any services that will not be provided that may be assumed to be included, and any additional services they believe are needed and that they can provide.
Supplier's team	An organigram to show how their team will function, with a summary of each person's role and responsibilities with interfaces to our team.
Conflicts of interest	Any conflicts of interest likely to pre-exist or arise.
Risks	An assessment of what the supplier considers to be the three key risks to the project and how they propose to mitigate them.
Inclusion	How the supplier will ensure that our inclusivity aims will be achieved.
Sustainability	How the supplier will ensure that our sustainability aims will be achieved.
Case studies	Three case studies (one page for each) that the supplier considers to be similar to this assignment with regard to the scale and challenge, including their relevance, and how the supplier (successfully) delivered them.
Programme	A programme for completion of the assignment and any critical key decision points/phase gates we need to be aware of and contribute to.
Commercial	The fee proposal for this project. Details of any exclusions and reasons for not being included.
Contractual and governance	The proposed form of contract and preferred governance structure to ensure we receive best value.
Appendices	A short biography for each of the team the suppler proposes for the assignment.

Tenders take time and cost money for the suppliers, so we should always be genuine in our request for proposals. We mustn't forget, in releasing an RFP, we're also presenting ourselves to the commercial property market; we'll be judged on our professionalism as a client, too. We should never think we're too cool a brand or too big an organisation to be rejected by the market; this really does happen!

1   **Evaluation**: we need to agree what we're assessing the suppliers on, prepare a standard form to document it, and agree internally who'll be involved. This should include a detailed review of responses, together with an interview and/or presentation. All members of our team must have read the RFP responses by the time the interviews happen – this is not just respectful but should ensure the best outcome.

2   **Decision** and **notification**: Once final, our decision should remain final and be clearly communicated as such. Beware getting into a 'bidding war' – it suits no-one and will compromise the integrity of both the process and our organisation. There should be a clear start date for the project that should be adhered to.

3   **Appointment**: having gone through the hard work, we can't then flail around with our contractual and payment terms or spend weeks running up a huge legal bill. Hence declaring any terms that may deviate from industry norms. Negotiating payment terms can be the most frustrating aspect for everyone and can sour a relationship before it's begun.

At this stage we also need to decide whether (or not) to a **non-disclosure agreement** (NDA) for bidding parties and successful suppliers. This may be dictated by organisational policy, as in, it's a given. If not, the following is a useful guide:

•   Use an NDA during the procurement process until such time that all key contracts are signed (especially a building lease) so as not to give away a negotiating position; but

- When the tender process is complete, formally release all those firms who signed an NDA from their obligations. The formal release is very rarely practised. Word of our final appointment will get out to the market anyway and will likely be deemed 'public domain' by this point.

WHO'S ON OUR PROJECT TEAM?

When we've assembled our internal stakeholders and external advisers, we'll have our full project team. The team needs to be inclusive enough to ensure all bases are covered, and yet not too big that we can't get anything done. It's also dictated to a degree by the construction choice we've made.

That said, it'll look something like Figure 4.3 (we're the project leader).

It's vital at this stage not to underestimate the need for effective **coordination** among the team. Regular meetings combined with the use of collaborative tools will be needed to achieve this.

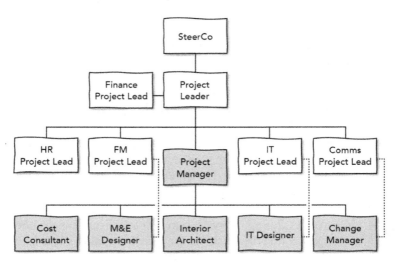

Figure 4.3 Typical project delivery team.

WHAT MEETINGS WILL BE NEEDED?

The following should likely (but not definitively) form the pattern of our regular coordination interactions. Sequencing will need some thought so that questions or issues from one type of meeting can be addressed soon after by another.

- **Core team**: these can potentially be weekly 'pulse' meetings, that are short with specific issues arising to cover or decisions required.
- **Project team**: the key project leads from the team shown above, probably monthly, chaired by the Project Manager with a pre-set agenda.
- **Workstreams**: the key functions will have a lot of technical matters to progress, including design, M&E, IT and change/communications. These are likely to be weekly meetings – and some of the core team will need to be included in some or all of them.
- **SteerCo**: the decision-making group of senior stakeholders covered earlier.
- **Change leads**: our colleagues who will manage information flow to and from our colleagues, who might meet fortnightly or monthly, depending on the scope of their activity. More on this role is covered below.

HOW WILL WE GET OUR COLLEAGUES INVOLVED?

At this stage, a small number of our colleagues have been involved – some within the core team, some as supporters and a SteerCo. A wider group of representatives from the organisation can now be brought in as a key channel of information to and from the project team. We often call this group 'change leads' or 'change champions'. We'll use **change leads** here. Beware choosing clever names that won't mean anything to our colleagues.

They'll sit within our 'supporters' strata, outlined at the start of this chapter. They'll be the essential channel between all colleagues who will use our new workspace and the core team, carrying news to colleagues, and insight and requests back to the team. A kick-off workshop is recommended, to align the change leads with the aims of the project. Thereafter, the role will require a meeting every fortnight or month, continual dialogue through open collaboration channels plus some time with their colleagues – so probably a total commitment of around half a day a month at most.

A rough order of scale – but certainly not a scientific measure – is one change lead per 25–50 colleagues (or one per department, neighbourhood, floor or physical area), depending on the nature and structure of the organisation. So, as a rule of thumb, a workspace that will house 500 people might need to involve around 15 change leads.

Our change leads should be influential, well-networked and regularly present colleagues, spanning different backgrounds, gender and age. It's preferable that they volunteer for the role. While they're expected to positively represent the creation of the new workspace, they may be sceptical or have doubts. That's fine – we're not looking for a group of 'yes people'; we're looking for those who care about creating a fantastic workspace. Constructive challenge from the change leads will be very helpful.

The change leads will have specific things to do. They should ideally be involved in the finalisation of the design, the selection of colours and fabrics, input to the design of collaboration spaces and the selection of furniture etc. within overall parameters approved by SteerCo. They should also be asked to review project communications before they're published and provide thoughts on behaviours in the new workspace.

TRUE STORY

The move to a new headquarters buzzed with anticipation at a thriving organisation, envisioned as a vibrant embodiment of the popular brand. The design, featuring a spectacular slide for whisking staff between floors, was shrouded in secrecy to amplify the wow factor of move-in day. The grand unveiling was spectacular, crowned with a rooftop terrace party. But the sparkle soon went flat. The 'wow!' became 'hmmm' as the layout perplexed colleagues. What was meant to be a dynamic workspace started to feel like a trophy cabinet for the project team. Involving our colleagues in the creation of their workspace isn't an option, it's a necessity. Or we may just end up with a glitzy party space rather than a fantastic place to work.

HOW MUCH TIME WILL WE NEED?

Time and money will of course both depend entirely on the size and scope of the new workspace.

A workspace project may finish under budget, either due to excellent sourcing or the budget being too generous. However, whether due to supply chain issues, slow decision making, changes of mind, cost cutting, design co-ordination issues or accidents – among many other probable causes – a workspace project (almost) never finishes early. In fact, credible research exists showing that over 90% of complex projects fail to deliver on time, on budget or both, because we constantly under-estimate the time needed to complete a task. Even when we've done the same thing before! It's known as 'planning bias'.

As another general rule, re-work usually takes longer than work and is rarely without cost and programme impact on other areas of the project, with dependencies only growing more complex as we progress.

There are standard 'build times' for construction, which a project manager will advise on. The fit-out of a floor of a typical office building will usually take approximately 14–16 weeks to construct and furnish, depending on location and market conditions. Where we have more than one floor, the times will overlap, to reflect specialist trades moving between floors. Two floors may therefore take around 18–20 weeks.

But this isn't the whole schedule, of course. There are also **lead-in** (at the beginning) and **readiness** (at the end) phases to consider. The lead-in phase will cover procurement time, order placement and the negotiation of terms, among others. It's a

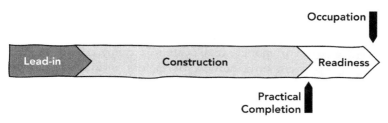

Figure 4.4 Typical overall construction schedule.

difficult period to estimate, but it does serve to stress once again the need to build in time expectations to include everything we've covered so far.

The **readiness** phase – covered in more detail in Part III – will start at the formal end of building work, termed **practical completion** (PC), when the site is handed over to our organisation by the general contractor. It includes stocking, testing and familiarisation through to the day that our colleagues pitch up to work for the first time. It's likely we'll be under pressure from our SteerCo to get into the new workspace as soon as possible, but we'll need at least two weeks for it and should hold firm on this period.

If we're renovating an existing workspace, moving colleagues out partially or in total, either to home or temporary ('**swing**') space, we'll also need to factor in time for this, too. If the works are being conducted in phases, we'll need lead-in and readiness time for each phase.

Although we're unlikely to predict exact timings, having timeframes like the ones we've shared provide a little positive pressure on programme as it focusses the team to pull together to ensure success, and the SteerCo on making timely decisions. No timeframes mean a greater propensity for time and scope drift.

HOW MUCH MONEY WILL WE NEED?

At this stage, we're budgeting. The cost plan comes later, when we've designed something and have a clear expectation of what we're likely to commit to spending. As nothing has been designed yet, we'll need to rely on advice from our external cost consultant and project manager based on their knowledge of similar design schemes and typical market rates.

The amount of money we allocate to creating our workspace will be dependent on a number of factors, including (but not restricted to):

- The **condition** in which we take our building – shell and core, Category A, Category B or, as is often the case, a mix of all three.

- The length of **commitment** we're making to the workspace – we may well decide to spend more if we're committed to stay for a lengthy period of time.
- The degree of **re-use** we deploy – principally IT equipment and furniture, and anything left behind by the previous occupants.
- Our level of **aspiration**, either for this workspace alone or as it relates to other locations in our portfolio. This may be related to the degree to which this workspace is 'customer facing', or how much of an internal message we wish to send.
- The degree of **sustainability** required – generally the 'greener' the workspace, the more expensive it will be (although at the time of writing, refreshingly this is starting to change).
- Our **procuremen**t strategy – whether we have global (or group) supply agreements in place or whether we choose to buy from smaller, local (or independent) suppliers.
- The broader **economic environment**, as it affects the supply chain, cost inflation or levels of uncertainty.

Just like the two approaches to specifying how much space we need, there are two approaches to budgeting:

- A **build-up** of what we think we'll need from zero, based on the description of what we want; or
- A given **pot of cash** from which we'll need to work out what we can afford to create our new workspace.

The reality is usually a bit of both. There are several key things to remember about budgeting:

- There's usually a **gap** between what we hope for and what we can afford. This is completely understandable, as most of the SteerCo probably won't have ever bought a new workspace before.
- Money doesn't **guarantee** success. An open purse can set unnecessarily high expectations from our colleagues, often resulting in an excessive, imbalanced or irrelevant outcome, which doesn't benefit anyone!

TRUE STORY

A workspace scheme, following concept design, just wasn't firing the imagination of the organisation's SteerCo. A new designer was brought in from within the interior architect firm to push the boundaries creatively. The revised design included amazing futuristic floor-to-ceiling (double height) blades at angles within the reception area, complete with edge lighting. The blades were costed and presented to the SteerCo. The chair of the SteerCo asked: 'Does the cost seem right for edge-lit floor to ceiling blades to you?', in reply to which they were met with a sea of blank looks. Everyone, however, on the SteerCo wanted them included. The cost of something never seen before can be incredibly difficult to estimate. It often comes down to a question of value.

- **Contingency** is essential, as with our programme. The authors have too many examples from their careers of a mistaken belief too early in the project that everything is agreed and known, and so costs can be too. A level of between 5-10% will be required, dependent on scale, to cover things such as:
  - Design co-ordination issues
  - Unknown (but now revealed) base building conditions
  - Supply chain issues, such as product availability
  - Design errors and omissions
  - Cost inflation
  - Product or service substitutions
  - Changes we may wish to make.
- Nothing is **excluded** – if its needed, it'll have to be paid for. The cost consultant will usually only set out the items within their control and view. They'll help with professional services, build, IT and furniture costs, but not items deemed to be ours (usually termed '**client direct**'). We always need to check a budget spreadsheet submitted to us for the list of 'exclusions' in the small print at the bottom. The simple rule in our budget is: if it needs to be spent, regardless of who is spending it, it should be included. This may mean estimating sums we need

ourselves or seeking input from our colleagues. Typical direct items include:

o   Furniture
o   Desktop IT
o   IT equipment upgrades
o   Printers
o   Internal plants
o   Signage and wayfinding
o   Branding
o   Fire extinguishers
o   Change and communications materials
o   'Magic touches' – the props, artwork, furnishings – stuff – that adds personality and meaning to make the space our own.

•   We'll need to **hold some money back** for the early months post move-in – not to be confused with snagging, which is covered in Part III. There'll likely be a financial exhaustion on the part of our SteerCo by the time final accounts are being settled, so asking for more at that stage will likely be met with a flat refusal. Unless, that is, we retain an amount in recognition that some things will need to be re-visited and changed. Around 5% of the budget for post-completion evolution of the workspace, as we shall cover in Part III, is incredibly useful. This may seem excessive at this stage but will pay dividends later.

Just as with time, a little pressure on cost can focus the team on design excellence rather than material indulgence. Refreshingly, there's now a higher value placed on frugality and environmental and social responsibility than we saw pre-pandemic. We're being challenged to do more for less. Often the result is both more creative and more appropriate for our needs.

THINGS TO LOOK OUT FOR

Here are some things to look out for in this area, to challenge or avoid:

•   **'Why don't we just DIY?'** As in: 'Why bother buying the services of professional, who just want to take our money and get away as fast as possible while doing the bare minimum?' Of course, we'll always do *some* things ourselves, but we'll face some internal pressure to minimise the number of professional advisers we use and then opt for the lowest cost when they're reluctantly accepted. But this is a false economy. Creating a great workspace requires the participation of a talented, motivated, experienced and high-performing team from the outset. Brilliantly led, of course.

- **'Our USP is ...'** We will, when buying professionals services, struggle to hear anything remotely approaching a 'unique selling point' (USP) from any firm in any given field. Processes are so well established across the industry in each case that the ultimate differentiator will very often be the people proposed for the project. Which means meeting those likely to be assigned to our project before they're appointed is vital.

- **'We don't need a change manager** (yet), it's a cost we can avoid.' Just as value in a workspace project is seen as tangible output, value in professional services is seen as technical output. Yet we somehow don't apply this to change advice and punt it downfield at our peril. If we're even having this conversation at this stage, they're already late being appointed.

5

LOCATE

HOW CAN WE FIND THE WORKSPACE
WE NEED?

This short chapter is a 'cut out and keep' for use in the event of a relocation. That said, even if we're simply renovating our existing workspace, the extension or renewal of a lease should be viewed in a similar way to a relocation. That is, as an opportunity to secure favourable financial terms from the landlord and a cost contribution to our project in exchange for our commitment to stay.

WHERE DO WE NEED OUR WORKSPACE TO BE?

There are two key challenges in finding new workspace – where and what.

In selecting a geographical location – a discipline often known as **site selection** – there are several factors to consider. Unless of course we know exactly where we want or need to be (hopefully the two are the same). The factors will change over time, too, so an awareness of trends will be important as we're likely to be in our new workspace for a while. They include:

DOI: 10.4324/9781003442684-7

1 **Human factors**:
   a. Existing talent – people already within the organisation
   b. Talent availability – people employed by other organisations, and those emerging from education
   c. Quality of life – schools, homes, recreation and safety
   d. Cost of living
   e. Labour costs and flexibility
   f. Connectivity – air, road and rail.

2 **Commercial factors**:
   a. Relocation costs and logistics
   b. Incentives and taxes (including how long any proposed arrangements will last)
   c. Proximity and access (not always the same!) to suppliers and customers
   d. Economic performance of the area
   e. Commercial real estate costs and availability.

If we're looking to move to a different country to our existing, there are a raft of other commercial, societal and political factors to consider, too.

When the location is confirmed, we'll need workspace.

WHO CAN HELP US FIND THE WORKSPACE WE NEED?

Although we can do the search ourselves, often engaging the services of a professional to guide a building search and negotiate the deal gets the best outcome. There are two types of representatives – the real estate market will dictate which type we'll work with due to what's available and who represents the spaces we're interested in. Each has advantages and disadvantages:

• **Agent**: an adviser who will represent 'us' in the commercial real estate market and try to obtain the best terms for us – they'll generally charge us a fee for their services, (the scale and calculation method differs by real estate market). With an agent, we get independence, but a potentially adversarial approach in negotiations with a landlord; or

- **Broker**: An adviser who represents 'the deal' – they bring both parties together to 'broker' (arrange) a mutually beneficial outcome and receive a fee for doing so from both parties. We lose independence but may gain a more collaborative approach.

HOW DO WE SELECT OUR WORKSPACE?

As with the workspace itself, it's always worth setting out what we want from a location to ensure an effective and well-targeted search. Factors we might consider and document include:

Aspect	*Considerations*
Specific location	Taking the 'site selection' location down to a specific area.
Space required	This was covered in Part I of the book.
Budget	Advice will often be required on market rates to set a 'per sq m/sq ft' (square metre / square feet) rental budget. It's also important to understand likely exposure to service charges and unrecoverable local taxes (see below).
Commitment	The length of contract we want – this is not always possible or may require a degree of compromise to achieve. The terms of any proposed breaks in the commitment should be clearly outlined and understood. Flexibility is considered in more detail below.
Grade	The standard of quality of building – for office (vs industrial) occupiers it's usually a choice between high (grade A) and medium (grade B).
Availability	Timing can be everything – albeit in the hybrid age, a period of working from home from the closure of existing workspace to the opening of the new is now entirely possible.
New or refurbished	Just as the re-use of furniture and technology is seen as a positive environmental message, so is the occupation of a refurbished building.
Age	Building plant and systems (e.g. power, exhaust, heating and cooling) tend to last 20–25 years before needing wholesale replacement. Other key areas of deterioration include the façade and glazing.

(Continued)

(Continued)

Aspect	Considerations
Environmental	The performance and accreditation related to construction and energy in use.
Style and image	The sophistication of steel and glass, or the charm of real brick? We must consider what's appropriate for our organisation, culture, values and how it'll reflect on us.
Building services	Effective ventilation is vital in the post-pandemic era – a minimum of five air changes per hours (ACH) is recommended (this may be subject to change) – with effective carbon dioxide monitoring offering a low-cost guide to air quality.
Sole or multi-tenancy	There are advantages and disadvantages of each. Multi-tenanted buildings provide potential flexibility to add or remove space but bring neighbours (and not always beneficial ones). Sole tenancies being the opposite of each.
Floor sizes	Unless there's a particular need not to, it's most beneficial for a workspace to be located on a single contiguous floor to maximise the possibilities for interaction.
Floor shape	Square or 'squat' rectangular shapes provide the greatest opportunity for organic layout and design. Longer, thinner 'corridors' allow for arrays of rooms or private offices. Odd or indulgent architectural shapes usually simply mean wasted space and hence unnecessary cost.
Floor to ceiling heights	Air space adds a greater sense of spaciousness even where floorspace is limited and aids acoustic performance.
Daylight penetration	Daylight is essential for human cognitive performance – however it's possible to go too far the wrong way; too much daylight can create glare, necessitating the use of blinds. Also, the more glass on the façade of a building, the greater the cost of heating and cooling often resulting in worse environmental credentials.
Cores	The building core contains stair access, lifts, washrooms and 'risers' (the vertical passages housing cables and pipes). The number and position of cores will impact workspace layout, circulation and daily operation.

Aspect	*Considerations*
Position in building	Higher floors often attract a rental premium and can be smaller than lower floors. Higher floors also need lifts that work – ineffective or too few lifts can cause delay and frustration getting in and out of the workspace.
Outside space	Roof terraces, balconies (particularly when covered) and garden spaces are often highly valued by our colleagues, and in most city centres remain a scarce offering.
Shared amenities	Landlords and developers are increasingly expected to provide shared amenities such as catering outlets, lounges, health and wellbeing facilities, cycle parking and showers. The provision of amenities will be reflected in the service charge shared by tenants.
Parking	The provision and allocation of dedicated or shared spaces or those available within local facilities at preferential rates.
Neighbours	Whether up or down with the building, or in adjacent buildings, it's important to understand who the neighbouring organisations are. Better to locate close to an organisation that shares similar values if possible, although it's difficult to know who might move in next door in future.
Roof space	Technology such as satellite dishes may require roof space and riser access.
Signage rights	We may wish to have a sign on the exterior of the building – or if we're taking the whole or majority of the space, possibly even naming rights. Certainly at the entrance to our workspace.

The **flexibility** of lease terms – who can break the lease, when and what conditions may apply – was always a contentious point of negotiation pre-pandemic: tenants wanted more, landlords less. In markets where terms are not prescribed by law, with variable patterns of attendance and less certainty of demand, flexibility has become even more important to us as tenants. The advice remains clear: secure as much tenant-only flexibility with as few conditions as possible at the outset. A lower rent for a longer commitment may appear attractive in the first instance, but there will be many more years over which to regret it.

HOW DO WE ESTIMATE WORKSPACE COSTS?

The sum of the below represents the **running costs** of a building. Unfortunately, it's often only the rent that attracts (or is brought to) our attention, yet this can represent less than half the total cost! We need to make sure we understand the following costs:

- **Rent**: charged by the landlord on the agreed 'net lettable' area shown in the lease. It may be necessary to have the area measured by an objective third party. Depending on the lease length and prevailing law and practice in the location, the lease will often include a mechanism to review the rent at certain intervals, but rarely to reduce it!
- **Service charge**: a proportionate share of the costs of common services, or 'amenities', provided in the building (e.g. reception and security) including insurance, some/all utilities (some may be separately metred), and maintenance of common parts and systems. The more amenities provided, the higher the charge is likely to be. The charges are usually reviewed annually.
- **Taxes**: locally levied taxes on real estate such as business rates in the UK. Sometimes they are complex to the extent that they are only understood by specialist professional advisers.
- **Operating costs**: the costs incurred directly for operating the overall workspace, such as: heating and cooling, lighting, maintenance, catering, cleaning and security. Management of these 'Facilities' (which is how we get FM – facilities management) will be covered in more detail in Part III.
- **Consumables**: the items we need for the day-to-day operation within our workspace based on usage, such as: IT networks, mail, stationery and print.

Landlords may either retain and manage their own properties, or outsource to a **managing agent** to administer the lease on their behalf, collecting rent and service charges as well as managing the services and common areas. This relationship can vary in quality from a few letters, service charge statements, an annual inspection and a ticking off for a minor lease transgression or two, to a full and fruitful dialogue. It's worth establishing the likely nature of the relationship, and thinking about what's best for us, before committing to a lease.

WHAT CONDITION WILL OUR NEW WORKSPACE BE IN?

Buildings are available in a variety of conditions reflecting the degree to which the space is ready for people to work in. We need to know this, as we'll have to complete (and pay for) the rest. The types are:

- **Shell and core**: the basic level of a building including its viable and watertight structure and floors (shell) and core(s) including lifts, stairs and vertical risers with key services (electrical, water and drainage).
- **Shell, core and floor**: the above plus a fully fitted raised access floor.
- **Category A**: the above plus ceilings and lighting, floor surfaces, mechanical and electrical services, fire detection, internal surface finishes and (sometimes) window blinds.

If we take a space from shell and core, it'll take more time and money to fit it out for our occupation. There's usually a financial contribution from the landlord for the Category A element of our fit out, but (while this may be contentious) it's rarely sufficient to cover the actual cost of it.

It's worth defining the other categories of completeness at this stage, as since the pandemic it's become more common to see space offered for rent in a fully habitable condition. These are usually the works and installations we must complete and pay for, covered later in Part Two of this book:

- **Category B**: the above, plus all built and operable spaces, including meeting rooms, offices, kitchenettes, technology infrastructure, storage, reception and other specialist areas.
- **Category C**: the above, plus the furniture, fixtures, audio visual (AV) and other equipment, branding, signage and wayfinding, planting and the like that goes into the space to make it work. Sometimes this category is included within Category B, as it's often difficult to separate B and C precisely.

HOW DO WE MANAGE THE REAL ESTATE TRANSACTION?

A real estate transaction is an activity that will result in a binding legal agreement, potentially several. It's worth stating that none of what follows constitutes legal advice but is related to the experience of managing the transaction process. We'll need to get local legal advice for the transaction.

The path is usually as follows, recognising that in different geographies the approach will vary:

1   Commission an **agent** or **broker**: agreeing a fee, usually stated as a percentage of the final value of the first year's rental. It's worth deciding before any enquiries begin whether the search (below) will be conducted under conditions of confidentiality.
2   **Search**: most agents/brokers access the same available market information, but some may become aware of 'off market' (yet unadvertised) opportunities through their contacts. A report of what is available at the time of search will be presented to us.
3   We'll need to agree a **long list** of the properties we think are worth further enquiry and perhaps visiting. We should use our criteria to focus in on the properties we think will fit best, but also allow for a few outliers to test our criteria, or it there's a specific feature we'd not thought about that we want to check out.
4   **Site visits**: assuming of course they are built, going to see the potential spaces is invaluable, as we can experience what it's

like to get to the location, the approach to the building itself and see what the surrounding neighbourhood is like. It's worth lining up a few in the same day, morning or afternoon to give a good sense of comparison. As a rule of thumb, around 5-8 sites to visit will give a flavour of what's available. In the case of new builds, the 'visit' may be to a marketing suite with an architectural model on display.

5   We'll then agree a **shortlist** of 3–5 potential candidates (assuming there are that many available – some areas may be more restricted or our needs very specific).

6   **Offers** on the spaces in which we're seriously interested will be requested from the landlords by our agents or brokers. It's always worth using a consistent set of questions for landlords to answer to help us compare 'like for like' – and to make the question set detailed. This can avoid later frustration from misunderstandings, or 'I didn't realise …' type missing information.

7   We then select our **preferred option** for final **negotiation of terms**. We should keep an acceptable second option in case anything goes wrong with the first. At this stage, our Project Manager (and their team) will examine the detail of the **building specification** to ensure we understand exactly what's being offered and conduct the appropriate **technical due diligence**. Our Interior Architect may prepare some **test fits** to ensure we can effectively occupy the space offered. Note these aren't 'designs' and so we need to be careful not to circulate them too widely in case they're misunderstood as such.

8   **Heads of terms**: the key commercial terms are agreed on the preferred option. As with the offers at (6), it's recommended that these are detailed as this will avoid lengthy and costly negotiations conducted by our lawyers.

9   **Lease negotiations**: in which the lawyers of each party talk to one another on matters of finer detail, usually within a reasonable period of exclusivity, which when finished will result in a minimum of two agreements:

a.   **Agreement for lease** (AfL): a promise to lease the space when the fitting out is complete and fully approved by the landlord and any statutory authorities, thus governing the terms of such – and containing:

b. **Lease agreement**: the actual lease that begins when (a) expires and the space is legally ready for occupation.

The last agreement we'll need will be the permission by the landlord for us to fit out the space as we've designed it, called (depending on location) a **licence to alter** (LTA). The landlord will levy a fee for reviewing and commenting on our design and granting permission, as their professional team will need to give their view. We can only agree the LTA when the design is complete, so if there are significant things we'd like to do (such as a connecting stair between floors), we'll need to get these approved in principle as early as possible. Early and open dialogue is vital, including the sharing of the design with the landlord at each stage.

During our negotiations, we'll have agreed the condition in which we'll need to return the space when we leave (often called **dilapidations**). The norm for dilapidations varies by country, but essentially, we need to try and minimise our liability to return the space into any kind of specific condition.

It should be noted that while this process has been laid out neatly and logically, moving workspace – like moving house – can be a traumatic experience if we're not organised, efficient and timely. Here are a few things we can do to mitigate the risks:

1   **Start early**. It's never too early to assemble our brief and start looking, even if it's too early at the time to transact. Keeping our cards close to our chests is important though; we don't want to commit to anything too soon!

2   Understand fully and clearly the **leaving requirements** for our existing workspace, to make sure we don't miss a lease break opportunity, don't get hit with a huge cost and aren't required to allow time to complete works before handing the space back.

3   Set out all key dates and actions on a **timeline** to make sure we don't miss anything, with all options and scenarios in one place. There will be critical 'go' or 'no-go' moments that we'll need to prepare ourselves for. Our project manager can help with this.

4   Get our **advisers** on board and internal approvals complete 'in principle' so we're ready to trade.

5   Find the **legal entity** within our organisation that'll be signing legal documentation. This often only applies to larger organisations, (we might need to draft in external help) but proceeding without it could become a potential trip hazard, as landlords will want a commitment from the most secure and stable entity possible. The matter of 'parent company guarantees' can often be contentious.

6   Research the commercial real estate **market** – costs, availability, developments. Everything we need to know that's relevant to our needs. As Sun Tzu said over 2,000 years ago, reconnaissance is seldom wasted.

7   Manage our **options** carefully at every stage, never leaving ourselves without a Plan B and C. One of our options may be to stay in our existing workspace, hence needing to complete (3) above. Or to acquire a smaller space than planned and supplement with flexible space or coworking. Which means being prepared to walk away from one or more opportunities if necessary.

8   Conduct thorough **due diligence** on our preferred options with our project manager and professional team, so we understand the nature of the buildings and workspace, what's in them and how they work. What we see on the outside can mask a lot beneath the floors, above the ceilings and in the walls. There's a cost to doing so, so it needs to be carried out on only those options on our short list.

9   Obtain as much **information** at offer stage as possible. One side of paper with the rent, lease length and little else will mean long, expensive and risky negotiations.

When we've secured our space, the real fun begins: we're ready to design our new workspace.

THINGS TO LOOK OUT FOR

Here are some things to look out for in this area, to challenge or avoid. Typically, we'll hear this from agents, brokers and landlords.

1   **'The space needs to be fitted out to Category A'** – so tenants can visualise how it'll look. The real estate market has been claiming this for many decades. Less than sufficient allowances for the Category A element in a lease deal reflects this. But when taking space fitted to Category A, tenants often end up stripping out much of what's been installed, as the design rarely fits the organisation's functional needs or finishes and materials preferences completely. Interior Architects can always help with visualising space presented as 'shell and core' and environmentally it's far more responsible.

2   **'We have no conflicts of interest.'** On the contrary, conflicts of interest are everywhere. The real estate market in any country is a web of relationships, predispositions and preferences. Most won't be visible or declared. That's not a criticism, just how it is. Real estate markets continue to function, and many are satisfied with the outcomes. But we need to always maintain a healthy scepticism and use our professional advisers to present objective facts for our decision.

6

DESIGN
WHAT WILL OUR NEW WORKSPACE BE LIKE?

We're around halfway through this book and we still don't know what our new workspace is going to be like! Which, let's face it, is the part most of us are interested in from the earliest inkling that there may be a workspace project on the horizon. But we're now ready to roll.

WHAT ARE THE STAGES OF THE DESIGN PROCESS?

Workspace creation is a human activity. It's often therefore subject to competing tastes and ideas, together with differing interpretations of the present and views of how the future should be. Judgment is often emotive rather than evidence-based, and different roles within an organisation will have diverse needs of the workspace. This is why we've spent so much time understanding needs of our organisation and people. Sometimes it's a wonder anything gets designed at all! This is how we can ensure ours does.

DOI: 10.4324/9781003442684-8

It's worth remembering that this book doesn't intend to detail out the process of developing workspace strategy and design, but to act as a guide to managing and leading it.

Every workspace strategist and interior architect has a logical, sequential process they like to follow. These are the professionals likely to be most involved at this stage. Their processes are usually very similar, as they typically set out how to get from empty floorspace to a fully functional, engaging, sustainable, safe and healthy workspace.

Given that we have established our requirements in Part I, from here there are four incremental phases commonly understood to comprise workspace design. In most countries they are captured in architectural standards to ensure commonality of understanding. The standardised stages tend to be tied up in industry-speak, so here's a simplified version:

1 **Design brief**: a formal statement of what we want, created from all the research that we and our professional services partners have completed to this stage and that are covered in the remainder of Part II of this book. The design brief document might be created by us, our workplace strategists, interior architects, or a combination of two or more. It usually includes:

   a. Context: Organisation mission, vision, values and approach to work: who we are and why we're doing this.
   b. High-level aims and intended outcomes.
   c. The overall function and 'look' of the workspace, as discussed earlier in Part II.
   d. Space requirements – either at the stage we set out in Part I, before we searched for new workspace, or here as a validation of what we completed ourselves.
   e. A central 'big idea' (like a hub, high street, town square or central staircase – the range of possibilities is limited, so the list isn't extensive).
   f. Worksetting types and their respective proportions.
   g. Key amenities and services.

2 **Concept design**: early-stage rough ideas of how the design brief will be interpreted in reality, often created using fast-prototyping software, showing layouts, colours, finishes and

materials to be used, and a combination of mood boards, visual sketches, two-dimensional plans and simple (in some cases) three-dimensional computer-generated imagery (CGI).

3 **Technical design**: the detail, including final layouts, worksetting design, full finishes and materiality specification, and furniture specification. CGI, if used at this stage, will be high quality and life-like and may include animated walk-throughs, or even virtual reality (VR) – these are exciting, and great for communicating and testing some design elements, but not necessary.

4 **Construction drawings**: the design is detailed to a level to enable construction on site and the manufacture of bespoke installations such as joinery.

Unlike other, more iterative design processes that involve short cycles of prototyping, testing and tweaking such as in software or product development, workspace design often includes long lead times for thing to be procured and constructed. So, it's essentially a linear process with a sign-off (approval) at the end of each phase. As we progress, any changes made will progressively cost more and introduce more delay, which in turn increases costs. So, we've got to make sure we hold regular progress reviews, so that a whole lot of work doesn't get done that we don't like – and to be *really* sure we (and our stakeholders) are completely happy at each stage before progressing to the next.

We also need to remember that workspace design isn't just about interior architecture. We also need to design our mechanical and electrical (M&E) services. Their coordination with the interior architecture is vital, and a key responsibility of our project manager. At both design and construction stage, and in readying our workspace for occupation, coordination presents the greatest risk to our completing on time and budget.

WHAT ESSENTIAL DESIGN PRINCIPLES SHOULD WE APPLY?

Beyond the nuances and particular needs of every organisation in every workspace, in the view of the authors (appreciating others may have a different view) there are six overriding, universal design principles that should underpin the creation of every workspace, and against which we need to test all our decisions. These universal principles are achievable whatever our scope, scale or budget.

Sometimes pursuing one principle will demand a compromise with one or more of the others; the tension between each principle helps to create a balance that's right for us.

1 **Functionality**: the workspace is there to enable work and itself must work brilliantly. Which means it needs to be simple and intuitive enough for our colleagues to understand and use without instructions. Right down to the finest detail, which is often what people are most interested in. Our colleagues will 'sweat the small stuff' and so must we.

2 **Wellbeing**: our workspace is for human habitation, and so the needs – conscious and unconscious – of humans should be at its heart. The physical, emotional and cognitive wellbeing of our people helps them to perform better and feel more connected to our colleagues and the organisation. There are several things we can do to contribute to the wellbeing of our colleagues in our workspace, covered later in this section.

3 **Inclusivity**: our workspace should be open to access, use and enjoy equally by everyone. There's no formula for this but working with our equality, diversity and inclusion (ED&I) colleague(s) is a great place to start, and will help us to think through needs, work up options and refine detail. We cover some suggestions in this area later in this section.

4 **Sustainability**: we simply can't forge ahead with creating a new workspace without consideration for the environment, our impact on it must a principal consideration when building and (just as importantly) operating our workspace. As with inclusivity, we cover some suggestions in this area shortly, too.

5 **Balance**: extreme solutions rarely work or stand the test of time. While there can be a temptation to be as bold as possible, to push boundaries, and prompt a 'Wow!' reaction, workspace needs to balance the needs of everyone who uses it and enable the work they need to do. And they won't all want to do the same things in the same way at the same time.

6 **Flexibility**: we're creating something based on present (known) and future (predicted) needs. Our organisation will continue to

evolve, and its needs and the needs of everyone within it'll do so, too. Our workspace must be able to adapt over time to account for these changing needs – it's a journey, not a finished product.

TRUE STORY

One of the authors once attended a multimillion-dollar corporate training centre in the USA. It had the most incredible facilities, and the catering was outstanding. Yet the chatter at break times was about something else: the spectacle wipes in the washrooms. In each, by the handwash basins, was a dispenser with small, moist (and recyclable) wipes. The view of the management team being, given the cost of the training on offer, you should at least be able to see what was written on the screens. Small things, especially those that respond to an unarticulated need, can make a massive difference to how our colleagues feel about their workspace.

HOW DO WE THINK ABOUT THE OVERALL WORKSPACE EXPERIENCE?

As mentioned in the introduction to this book, workspace – comprising worksettings, amenities, technology and services – is just one aspect of the workplace.

There are other factors we can't necessarily control that will help create a fantastic place to work, such as the organisation's:

- Values
- Management ethos and practice
- Approach to equality, diversity and inclusion (ED&I)
- Learning and development pathways
- Career development or enrichment opportunities
- Reward and recognition structures
- Promotion of trust and openness
- Social commitments.

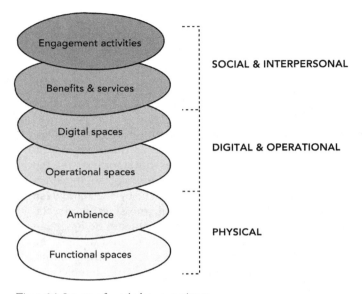

Figure 6.1 Layers of workplace experience.

Our purpose here is focussing on what we specifically *can* influence.

There are several layers of experience we can develop that together create a positive environment that enables work to get done and connections to be made. They comprise three main areas of focus, each comprising two layers (adapted from, and with thanks to, Timothy Ahrensbach at the LEGO Group):

- **Physical**
  - o **Functional** spaces designed to be used for departmental, individual, collaborative and social activities, where our colleagues can work alone and together, recharge, explore and connect with each other internally and externally.
  - o The **ambience** – the 'look and feel' that makes the workspace uniquely an expression of 'us' and reinforces what we care about through the choice of materials and finishes, and what we might call 'brilliant basics'.

- **Digital and operational**
  - **Operational spaces** include facility operations and services that are dependent on individuals and team needs as they evolve.
  - **Digital spaces** include tools that connect employees and resource across the organisation and with external partners, helping us work seamlessly whether within or outside the workspace.
- **Social and interpersonal**
  - **Benefits and services** including workspace amenities that bring people together, such as a coffee bar, meditation area and wellbeing services to help support mental and physical wellbeing.
  - Community-building and **engagement activities** such as programmed events – internal and for external guests – and organisation-wide celebrations that build connections, new skills, excitement and pride, like award ceremonies, brand experience spaces, and the like.

Paradoxically, claims of the positive contribution fantastic workspaces can make to an organisation and its people are often both overstated and under-estimated.

It's important to state, however, that a fantastic workspace won't fix an organisation's toxic culture. The other ingredients need to be in place, too, to create the best possible people experience.

WHAT SHOULD THE WORKSPACE SAY ABOUT US?

Whatever we do with our workspace, it's going to say something about our organisation, to both our colleagues occupying the space and visitors to it. Even to those who aren't present, through sharing on social networks and evaluation websites. It may scream. It may whisper. But it'll say something; we don't have a choice in the matter. The choices we make in the design of our workspaces – whether conscious or not – express things such as attention to detail, whether we care about wellbeing, how we make decisions and what we prioritise.

Post-pandemic, organisations in most countries are far more in tune with the way they're perceived than they perhaps once were, even those who aren't 'public facing'. While in some locations, projecting status is no longer considered necessary, this isn't universally true and is therefore market dependent. Nevertheless, the workspace should ideally reveal a balance between the intent to optimise the quality of the colleague experience with the need to be commercially and environmentally responsible.

It's possible, through its design, that a workspace can make a meaningful contribution, reinforcing that the organisation:

- **Cares** – about its people, community, customers and the planet.
- Is **prudent**, unwilling to waste or squander its resources, as reflected in the amount of workspace occupied, the way it's created and materials used.
- Does what it says it believes in, living and breathing its declared **values**. Not just putting them on a laminated poster in the cafe or (as was vogue for a time) painting them on the walls.
- Values the learning, **development** and growth of its people.

These contributions can be tricky to apply, as they might be argued for in several ways, so we need to exercise careful consideration and continually use our design principles as our guide.

TRUE STORY

When a B-Corp non-for-profit organisation decided to spruce up their space post-pandemic, their goal was an efficient, energising workplace, connecting people to both their colleagues and their altruistic mission. Enter the new head of buildings and facilities, a leader eager to blend nourishment with togetherness by reintroducing food services. Initial plans were met with cheers until the reveal: pre-packed sandwiches and plastic condiment sachets. These clashed glaringly with the company's dedication to health, nutrition, and sustainability. Rather than scrapping the plan entirely, a swift intervention was made. Colleagues were called upon to infuse the project with their insights, leading to an array of imaginative and sustainable food solutions: breakfast buffets, homestyle cereal and bread dispensers, and local food provided by social enterprises. The ketchup sachet debacle turned into a tasty reminder that even the simplest amenities can be steeped in meaning, mirroring the values of the organisation and its people.

WHAT DO WE WANT THE WORKSPACE TO LOOK LIKE?

The 'look' of the workspace will be developed during the design process. While no-one wants to be placed in a 'box' in respect of design, we may wish at this stage to have an agreed sense of the overall or predominant style we wish to see, to brief the designers. There are several typical design 'routes', or styles, outlined below. Given our organisation's personality and values, our outcome will probably be a unique blend of a few of the following:

- **Corporate**: simple, understated and functional, with sparing use of accents or flourishes. This is a common outcome, albeit not usually stated in a brief as it often results in a 'vanilla' space due to compromises made to meet various differing needs.
- **Classic**: richer colours and finishes such as deep greens, reds and gold, materials such as darker timber and 'above functional' fittings such as chandeliers. This 'traditional' style is firmly rooted in the offices of the industrial revolution, which typically echoed the Study or Library in posh houses (think the White House or a top-tier law firm).
- **Modern**: understated – crisp, clean lines, using materials such as steel, glass and light timber, set against a palette of white or subtle pale shades. Corbusier was an early pioneer; Swedish design, with its simple forms and 'honest' materials, is another expression of this style.

- **Bold**: a statement – strong, rich primary colours, defined lines and shapes, deep textures and contrasts. Think early Google playfulness.
- **Minimal**: economical in finishes and content, form created by light and shade, with plenty of 'white space'.
- **Industrial**: 'brutal' in the architectural sense – unfinished surfaces, reclaimed materials and furniture, and exposed brick, mechanical and electrical services.
- **Eco**: biophilic emphasis, with natural materials, woodland colour palette and circadian lighting.
- **Residential**: calm, relaxed, warm and familiar, a workspace that resembles home (or at least as Interior Architect's idea of home!) with soft furnishings, rugs and table lamps.
- **Creative**: think 'studio' – surfaces for brainstorming, 'play' materials, sofas and large tables for team working.
- **Eclectic**: intentionally 'mis-matched' or random styles, often with contrasting colours and textures that come together confidently to stimulate the sense. Typically used as an 'accent', restricted to certain spaces.

Often a series of workshops will help the Interior Architect get to know us better and help us to articulate both the overall theme of our workspace and also how the 'tone' of spaces might change depending on their use or the experience we want to create.

To help get us into the colours, textures and furniture elements, our Interior Architect will create **mood boards**, with pictures of other workspaces, to capture the essence and spirit of a look to help us decide what we like and want to see in our workspace. This information is easily available online should we wish to do it ourselves.

Of course, even though it's often the main focus of design, it's not just about what we see. Our other senses can be explored for their contribution, too, as retail and hospitality have done for many years:

- **Touch**: the textures of furniture, surface coverings and materials can soothe or stimulate. Installations and features that invite us to physically interact with them make for a more engaging experience. We're innately curious.

- **Sound**: not just a choice of radio station, sounds when 'scaped' can be calming and function as masking in more open environments (e.g. 'white noise'). There's a big difference between a calm space and one that's deathly quiet, just as a buzzy backdrop can be motivating whereas poor or absent acoustic baffling or the insensitive arrangement of worksettings can become intensely distracting.
- **Smell**: beyond fresh bread and coffee (lovely as they are), or nasty pine gels in the washrooms (not lovely at all), subtle scents, including those from living plants and natural materials can lower stress levels, create positive memories and associations.
- **Taste**: it's not likely that we'll be licking the furniture (hopefully), but this sense plays out in the quality of air; is it fresh or stale? Also, if there's a catering service, the variety and uniqueness of the offer can create a positive association with the workspace.

While not directly related to our senses, there are a few additional sensory considerations:

- **Spaciousness**: this is where we're thinking about and guiding the gathering of people and things. Extremes such as densely packed (battery farm) arrangements or a sea of open desks (ghost town) can be disorienting and demotivating. We need to balance 'line of sight' to colleagues and information with the need for privacy and separation.
- **Aliveness** or **movement**: this relates to the 'buzz' of a space – its energy – specifically, how people are channelled through spaces to create interest, reduce distraction and generate a feeling that things are happening; that there's life.

We're now going to consider all the component parts of our workspace in more detail:

- Worksettings
- Amenities

- Support facilities
- Building systems
- Technology.

WHAT WORKSETTINGS WILL WE NEED?

When thinking about the worksettings we'll need, much will depend on what our workspace is for. But balance will still likely be an overriding objective.

Before and after the pandemic, credible research and common good practice in workspace design has consistently supported the requirement for a roughly equal balance between worksettings for:

- **Solo work**: with varying degrees of focus required; and
- **Interaction**: planned and unplanned, formal and informal, involving varying numbers of people.

Yet there's also a middle ground: **proximity** to our colleagues, where we're working on our own tasks but within easy reach for unplanned conversation as required. Working in proximity means we can oscillate between solo and interactive work.

Worksettings will be needed to enable all three types of activity – solo, interactive and proximal. Some worksettings will specifically meet the needs of one type of activity, others will be able to support multiple. Of course, it's likely our colleagues will use the worksettings for whatever suits their needs, so it'll be important to note the difference between initial intent and actual use.

Essentially, there's a standard kit of parts comprising built structures, furniture and technology, that will suffice for most workspaces. They've been arranged below by work activity:

Figure 6.2 Modes of working.

Work activity	Activity	Worksetting	Description
Individual 'everyday' work	Solo Proximal	**Desk**	Flat surface for general work with monitor and peripherals (keyboard and mouse) – can be fixed (static) or height adjustable.
	Solo Proximal	**Touchdown**	Flat surface for general work – usually a bench or table with power but no monitor or peripherals.
Individual confidential or focussed work	Solo	**Focus desk**	Desk with three higher sides for acoustic/visual privacy with monitor and peripherals.
	Solo Interactive	**Private office**	Enclosed room for one or more person with desk(s) and perhaps meeting furniture.
Online meetings or calls (1–2 people, sound attenuated)	Solo	**Phone box**	Enclosed, sound attenuated room or furniture item, single seat or 'perch' and small table, for phone or web calls.
	Solo Interactive	**Pod**	Enclosed, sound attenuated room or furniture item with surface, for 1–3 people, for focussed work or calls.
Small non-confidential interactions (2–4 people)	Interactive	**Diner booth**	A pair of adjoined medium or high-backed sofas, open or closed at one end with a central working height table.
	Interactive	**Huddle table**	Standard seated or standing height table and chairs in open space.
Small confidential interactions (2–4 people)	Interactive	**Meeting room**	Enclosed room with table and chairs or soft seating, with monitor for web calls and presenting.

(*Continued*)

(Continued)

Work activity	Activity	Worksetting	Description
Large non-confidential interactions (5+ people)	Interactive	**Various**	Anywhere that works – meeting room, cafe or kitchen space.
Large confidential interactions (5+ people)	Interactive	**Meeting room**	Enclosed room with table and chairs or soft seating and monitor for web calls and presenting. May offer the potential for different table and seating settings (albeit while this sounds appealing, is far more difficult in practice!).
Social ('non-work') interactions	Interactive	**Cafe or kitchen area**	Area with tables, chairs, benches and spaces to stand.
Training		**Meeting room** (possibly modified)	Meeting room with particular types of furniture orientation, potentially reconfigurable, often with additional whiteboards and technical kit.
Client engagement	Interactive	**Lounge**	Area comprising work and social space for client use, including catering options (self-service or staffed), usually separated from general work areas.
Scrum	Interactive	**Desk** (where people sit back-to-back)	Layout of desks, wall boards and wall-mounted monitors suited to software engineers.
Stand-up	Interactive	**Scrum wall**	Magnetic whiteboard, with monitor(s), for short, standing, non-hierarchical meetings.
Trading	Interactive	**Desk**	Specialist layout for financial traders, usually densely packed with multiple screens per desk.

There may be variants on each, such as meeting rooms of differing sizes with different types and orientation of tables, and variations in design that create the sense of a wider range of worksettings. It's also worth noting that most worksettings are still oriented towards seating. Some of the settings listed can be supplemented with opportunities to stand, or perch, for all or some of the time. However, it's important to remember that standing worksettings may exclude those with some physical disabilities.

Other portable or non-portable free-standing items might also be added to the space including partition units (shelving with multiple inserts to delineate space), whiteboard units and wardrobes or coat stands.

TRUE STORY

One of the authors wrote a satirical blog post about an imaginary tech giant in whose workspace a meeting was taken in a gazebo – a device wholly pointless indoors. This caused much amusement at home, and for several years became the author's symbol of over-specifying worksettings. Later, the author attended a meeting at a prospective new client's London HQ, under construction. During the walk around, the project lead pointed to an area of the workspace and proudly stated: 'That's where the gazebo will be going.' Truth and satire aren't far away in our workspace. We should be wary of creating worksettings in a bid just to be different – the novelty will wear off quickly, and we'll be stuck with them.

HOW DO WE MANAGE REQUESTS SUCH AS: 'I WANT MY OWN DESK'?

There has been a slow and undeniable trend towards open, shared workspace and away from private offices and assigned desks for the last several decades. But it hasn't all been one-way traffic. There are still expectations of, and legitimate needs for, assigned space.

There may be several reasons for assigned space being requested:

- There's a specific need for **confidentiality**, and hence a private office may be required for some or all the time. We may have to do some groundwork and have some honest conversations to distinguish real need from personal preference, but there are likely to be some roles or situations that qualify.
- There's a **cultural expectation**. In some locations, for senior roles in particular, there may be an expectation from clients of the organisation and official representatives attending the workspace that a certain standard and type of accommodation is provided, particularly at a senior level. In some countries this is highly prescriptive. We need to be aware that what works in one location won't always work in others, and so researching local custom and practice is critical.
- A high level of attendance is **expected** by the organisation. Following the post-pandemic shake-up, shared worksettings became the norm as we adapted to working in other locations, and so presence wasn't guaranteed for the organisation. Yet there may still be instances where 100% attendance is standard (holidays and sickness leave excepted), either because the role can't be performed remotely, management require it (irrespective of whether we think it's a good idea or not) or because there's a cultural expectation of physical presence. In such instances, assigned space may be appropriate.

Separating the practical from the political may well be a challenge on our project. It'll be up to us to ask the right questions and be prepared to manage how we respond to requests that are genuine, and those that aren't. A word of caution: it can often be the case that establishing qualifying criteria for workspace assignment can worsen the situation. Far from adding clarity, these requirements can escalate emotion as they can sometimes expose inequality or lack of rationale. We'll learn what battles are worth fighting, and what aren't, as our project progresses.

WHAT FACTORS WILL WE NEED TO CONSIDER WITH OUR WORKSETTINGS?

Our workspace will combine the physical structure of the building and its key features with the worksettings we design and install, comprising built elements and furniture, and the mechanical and electrical systems and technology that make it work.

Worksettings need to support the types of work our colleagues engage in. Pre-pandemic the terms 'primary' (desks, essentially) and 'secondary' (all other) worksettings were used, but that categorisation has now lost much of its meaning, as the ways and places in which we work have shifted dramatically.

TRUE STORY

A large team of software engineers had a questionable approach to housekeeping. They'd dragged in whiteboards, piled non-standard kit on desks, and stuck strips of paper and tickets all over the walls. It appeared like the organisation's investment in new, modern workspace was being rejected. There was almost nothing the FM team could do to keep the space tidy. Following some open and honest conversations, the project team researched the agile methodology, in particular how it worked and what workspace was needed. At the first opportunity, the project team created a workspace entirely geared to the engineers' work methods. Some of the organisation's execs struggled with the outcome, but the engineers loved it. And because it was designed to suit, they kept it clean and tidy. We really do have to understand our colleagues and how they work.

Essentially, worksettings will need to be:

- **Specified**: their purpose, function, components, technology and quantity – a 'bill of requirements'.
- **Designed**: the interpretation of the specification for our workspace including look, finishes and materials.
- **Arranged**: their location in relation to the building architecture (including daylight) and to one another, so that they work alone and together, and create the desired flow of people in the workspace. We referenced this when looking at sensory considerations.

Each of these tasks will in turn need to consider several factors:

- **Acoustics**: ensuring that the space overall has sound-absorbing materials and isn't all hard surfaces, and that adjacent worksettings are acoustically separated to avoid them nullifying one another. For example, where two open meeting tables are arranged side by side, only one would only be useable at a time. This can be particularly problematic in workspace that's generally open plan.
- **Ergonomics**: physical comfort is a vital component of the wellbeing of our colleagues. It's been a recent trend for workspace design to suggest how long someone should remain at a worksetting by applying degrees of discomfort. But the authors would argue it's not for us, as designers and specifiers, to decide – all worksettings should be ergonomic, by default, leaving our colleagues to determine how long they need to stay.
- **Technology**: we'll need to consider the hardware that will be within or on the worksetting, paying particular attention to getting power and data to it, and strengthening walls where we need to hang screens.
- **Accessibility**: we listed inclusivity as key design principle, so we'll need to ensure that everyone can access and use every worksetting provided. High stools and tables, benches and banquette seating at tables can be problematic.

WHAT AMENITIES WILL WE NEED?

These are a mix of required, recommended and optional areas or features intended to meet a specific business, support or social purpose that add to the overall experience in the workspace. We may work in some of them (e.g. a cafe) but we don't count them as worksettings, as enabling work isn't their main purpose. Most are optional but can add tremendous value in terms of enabling social cohesion and wellbeing.

Those that are required (in the case of washrooms) or recommended include:

- **Washrooms**: in shared buildings they're sometimes in the landlord area and so not in scope, but where they are we must make sure they're treated as well as the rest of the workspace. They're often one of the two spaces – along with reception and meeting rooms – that our visitors will see – and so they say a huge amount about how we value our people. They also need to consider (but too often don't) the practicalities associated with this unique space. Creating fantastic washrooms is a project within a project.

- **Reception** or waiting area: preferably designed to encourage social interaction or informal work so it's not just a 'dead' space, with a designer sofa sitting on a fluffy rug. It's even better if this area has refreshments.
- **First aid room**: not always a legal requirement, but advisable to have.
- A **new mothers' room** can often be combined with a First Aid room in what is often termed a **wellbeing room**. It'll need ambient and relaxing décor, acoustic and visual privacy, localised temperature control, armchair, sink, various lighting settings, refrigerator (for very cold water) and a hand drier that is effective in helping to dry clothing, too. Importantly, it'll need to be secure from the inside with the possibility of external emergency access, have an emergency call point, and have an 'occupied' indicator externally. Priority access to this space should be given to new mothers, who may need to use it with little or no warning; therefore, it should not be bookable.
- **Multifaith room** (or quiet/contemplation, 'Zen'): These spaces are essential and needs to be thought through, not thrown in as a tick-box exercise. It should ideally be located in a quiet, private area, with similar ambience and privacy to the new mothers' room, but with enough floor space to lie down or stretch. It should be equipped with washing facilities, too. The frequency of use of this space varies depending on our colleagues, but often there will be a regular pattern of use. Careful understanding of who will use it and how is essential. It's worth noting that the value of this and the new mothers' room is not in high levels of occupancy, rather the provision of the space and the care and comfort it affords.
- **Kitchenette(s)**: a place to eat and drink, ideally with a bench or table and seating, fridge, microwave, tea and coffee and filtered water.

- **Cafe**: an enhanced social space with tea and coffee, possibly a barista service (if we're lucky!), various furniture options and everything found in a kitchenette.

Those that might be considered (if we have the space and budget) include:

- **Restaurant**: cold and possibly hot food. The latter requires far more back-of-house provision – such as catering-grade equipment, storage, washing and changing – that should be thoroughly checked by a catering consultant.
- **Tech 'bar'**: access to IT support and kit supply – ideally with a counter, storage, waiting and meeting areas. Long gone are the days when it's acceptable for the IT team to be hidden away in a cave, their support is the lifeblood of the organisation. Vending machines for standard consumables such as headsets and chargers are also increasingly useful and appreciated.
- **Demonstration area**: for the organisation's products or initiatives, with space for people to view, engage and ask questions.
- **Library**: an area designated for quiet or focussed work. Although hard-copy books are less common, a single place to access 'analogue' knowledge can be highly valued by our colleagues. We may also want to use such spaces to encourage 'offline' deep thinking and inspiration. Again, it's not about achieving a high density of occupation, but about the amenity being available for when needed.
- **Interview room**: often 'landside' (not behind security barriers) and discreet, for up to four people, where it's desirable not to have visitor 'sign in'.
- **Gym**: of any size and features. We'll need to consider the provision and proximity of shower, changing and locker facilities. It's also worth considering local amenities, as offering a subsidy may suffice and obviate the need to provide this ourselves.
- **Exercise room**: for specific activities such as yoga or Pilates – may have a sprung floor and mirrored wall.
- **Games room**: with relaxed furniture and gaming consoles.
- **Retail** (or retail pop-up): space and the means to display and sell goods.

When we've finished using them all, there may even be some time left in the day for work!

TRUE STORY

An organisation had a strong association with swimming as a sport. A benefactor financed the building of a 25 metre, five-lane swimming pool on its owned estate, connected to the office building. It was a beautiful facility. Of over 500 people working at the location, only five ever used the pool. No one had factored in the nervousness of being seen by colleagues in a swimsuit. It was used for photo shoots and marketing purposes, but for most of the day the water's surfaced remained unbroken. It's worth remembering that our work and personal lives have natural boundaries.

DO WE NEED TO CREATE NEIGHBOURHOODS?

We mentioned above that the arrangement of worksettings is incredibly important. In this regard the term 'neighbourhood' has become common, particularly those workspaces that are of the 'landscaped' variety. We may also refer to neighbourhoods as **zones**.

Just as with the urban environment, a neighbourhood is a defined, fixed physical area of a workspace, with a degree of identity. The identity may just be a name or helpful reference that enables us to orientate ourselves, through to a form of physical distinction like colours or finishes.

The approach is applied where we have a floorplate of a size that requires us to divide it up for it to make sense to the occupants, rather than simply create one large space.

Each neighbourhood should ideally have a similar mix of worksettings, as we'll often need to move quickly and easily between them during a typical working day. We may assign specific features to them, such as our tech bar or library, such that they become known for them.

It's advisable not to refer to the teams assigned to a particular space as a neighbourhood, as team size and composition will regularly change as the organisation changes. We'll consider the allocation of people to workspace in more detail Part III.

WHAT SUPPORT FACILITIES WILL WE NEED?

The spaces aren't either worksettings or amenities, but are vital to the effective operation of the workspace; they are what we call 'support' spaces or facilities:

- **Resource (copy) areas**: a semi-enclosed area usually with printer/photocopier (or multifunctional device, MFD), storage for stationery and work surfaces for collating documents and leaving/collecting mail. These areas can be noisy and so need to be positioned away from focus workspace.
- **Lockers**: banks of secure, personal storage units, 3–5 units high. They may be of varying sizes to suit different needs. Access can be via keys, punch-code locks or smartphone apps. They can be assigned or used as needed. More is said about lockers in Part III.
- **Storage**: secure on-floor cabinets for papers and other resources. A typical rate to apply might be 0.5–1 linear metre (1.6–3.5 linear feet) per person, which roughly equates to half to a single shelf of a standard size filing cabinet.
- **Storerooms**: there's always stuff to store – papers, archive material in transit, filming equipment, merchandise and usually a fire-proof safe. Perhaps even a chocolate fountain (a true story).
- **Equipment room**: for on-site servers and key IT equipment – usually locally and separately cooled, and sometimes with a local fire suppression system. There may also be a need for a separate **UPS room** (uninterrupted power supply) – our IT team can confirm, so we're best to ask early.
- **IT build room**: preparation and servicing of IT equipment (PCs and laptops), needing working height counters, storage beneath and plenty of power sockets.
- **Mail room**: incoming and outgoing mail handling – needing counter tops, paper and stationery storage, racking and potentially space and power for a franking machine.

- **Showers**: often found in the basement of shared buildings, where there may also be cyclist/runners' lockers. There may be a need to add 1–2 shower units within our workspace.
- **Cleaners' store**: storage of cleaning equipment, materials and consumables. The tiny on-floor 'closets' with a Butler sink provided within a main building are rarely sufficient to store materials.

Other support spaces might include: 'dry' workshop or maker space, or a 'dirty' workshop (with prototyping machines and equipment).

WHAT BUILDING SYSTEMS DO WE NEED?

While all aspects of our design are subject to compliance with regulations, this is particularly so with mechanical and electrical (M&E) systems. Non-compliance can mean we can't legally occupy the workspace, even if we think it's finished. Building systems we'll need to be aware of include:

- **Heating, ventilation and cooling** (HVAC) – including fresh air supply and humidity control.
- **Fire safety**: the degree to which the building can minimise the risks from fire, heat and smoke, ensure that occupants can evacuate as quickly and safely as possible, and emergency services can access the building where such events occur.
- **Utilities and energy**: matters related to the supply of electricity, gas and water, and the outflow of the latter including waste.
- **Power**: electrical supply and distribution.
- **Data**: the provision of sufficient high-speed fibre to the building itself and its distribution throughout the floors.
- **Lighting**: workspace, specialist and emergency lighting, often with sensing and control systems. It's often worth bringing in a specialist lighting designer to work closely with our interior architect and M&E designer as the outcomes are often well worth the investment both in terms of performance and ambience.

- **Access and security**: including closed circuit television (CCTV), access control and intruder detection. In a shared building the landlord will have a process including staff and a system to manage who is allowed entry. We'll probably have to use that system to get into the main building and may either be able to extend its use to our floor(s) or must procure and install our own with the guidance of our M&E designer. Asking colleagues and visitors to use two separate systems – possibly even two access cards or fobs – isn't a great experience, and so where it's possible to align them, we should seek to do so.
- **Building management system** (BMS): controls all the systems of a building to ensure they are healthy, safe and comfortable. In a shared building there may be two – one for the main building controlled by the landlord, and one for our workspace. Or we may have access to, and the ability to view or even control, conditions in our own workspace through the landlord's BMS.

As covered in Part I, regulations will vary by country, but the considerations above, when combined, form the basis of the **statutory maximum** number of occupants assigned to an area of a building, to ensure that it's not over-occupied and therefore unhealthy and/or unsafe. Factors considered in arriving at this number usually include fire, fresh air, ventilation and toilet provision.

An incredibly useful exercise to undertake when thinking about what building systems are required is to map **user journeys**. This approach is especially useful for access, security and visitor management systems, where their design is often modelled on people behaving sensibly and logically – which, of course, they sometimes don't. The user journey map can help us specify and better procure what we need.

We might also extend this user journey mapping to the approach to the whole experience of hybrid working – present and potential future – to test how our workspace supports our colleagues across a whole (and varied) week. These can be useful to show different use-cases and communicate new ways of using space, sometimes presented as 'day-in-the-life' illustrations (also covered in Part III).

WHAT TECHNOLOGY WILL WE NEED?

Technology in the workspace comprises four broad areas. The choices made in each area will be central to the design and operation of our workspace, so our IT team will need to be involved from the outset and remain so in this workstream throughout.

Connectivity

After health and safety considerations, high speed, highly reliable connectivity is probably the main requirement of any modern workspace. Whether it be via a cabled network (ethernet) or Wi-Fi – usually both – it must work, and work seamlessly, all the time. Or our colleagues will simply go elsewhere.

Connectivity also includes voice, mostly in the post-pandemic era via the internet and not a traditional wired desktop phone (PABX) system. Which means headphones, not handsets. Outside of contact centres and the like, most day-to-day voice communication will be over mobile telephones.

Desktop

We're likely to spend some of our time working from just a laptop, connected via Wi-Fi, where power will be the main cabled requirement. The general rule is, wherever it's possible to put power sockets, we should put them.

Sometimes we all need a large screen – or two – a keyboard and a mouse. So, we'll need to decide which desks have how many screens and what kit will be provided. If we're providing screens, we'll also need to agree whether we'll use adjustable arms or the stands they are supplied with.

It should be noted that there's usually a passionate and vocal lobby for dual screens on desks, as there's often a fear that it's a provision that will be removed. But not everyone wants or needs them. This means understanding the extent of the need and meeting it as required, rather than simply installing dual screens everywhere just in case.

The same is often true of privacy screens, sometimes requested in open plan workspace by colleagues working on confidential material. They're often not designed to be portable, so they don't lend themselves to an agile workspace. It's better to try and identify low-traffic areas as higher-confidentiality spaces, where desk screens can't be overlooked or seen in passing.

Presentation

Commonly termed 'AV' (audio visual) this includes all kit in meeting rooms and information screens we may site around our workspace (sometimes called 'digital signage'). Just as with connectivity, high quality and reliable AV is a modern expectation. Particularly when so many meetings involve participants who aren't physically in the room.

AV also needs to support the ability hold events – large gatherings or 'town halls'. Some or all this kit may be provided within our workspace, either fixed or immediately available, or if the frequency is low, rented as needed.

Applications

Much is made of the benefits of 'workspace technology', which generally refers to applications (apps), but the phrase is a huge catch-all. It's also an area where it's sometimes difficult as a buyer to understand what's being offered. It's not like choosing a desk, for example, where we just select a style, colour and cable management and compare prices. Sometimes the technology represents a whole new genre, offering to fix a problem we're not sure we even have.

Some applications require hardware installation, usually in the form of sensors or display/input screens that can be purchased or rented. These may include those monitoring environmental conditions, human presence or space booking.

It's certain that the world of workspace apps will continue to develop quickly, and so anything offered here may have moved on by the time you read this. We can break down the options into the following types that relate specifically to workspace:

- **Building management**: either linked to the BMS that governs temperature and humidity, among other things, or to types of sensors – or both – this technology regulates the environment and provides useful management information.

- **Concierge**: usually via a smartphone, these applications tell us what's going on within the organisation and locally and allow us to access amenities and services. They often link to standard organisational applications such as holiday and absence management.

- **Reservation**: a long-established practice, these rules-based applications allow us to reserve (book) things such as meeting rooms and desks. They often include 'check in/out' features providing management information – if colleagues use the application, of course. General workspace application suites also offer the ability to reserve spaces, and so a separate application may not be necessary.

- **Smart spatial scheduling**: a more recent genre of application that uses AI to help colleagues arrange time and space in which to work together. Invented by GoSpace AI, this technology uses proprietary artificial intelligence, AIDRA®, to optimise team working by predicting when and where a colleague may need workspace and who they need to work with and automatically placing teams in the right type and size of space. AIDRA® simultaneously ensures that the overall quantum of space made available matches the workforce's demand over-time, allowing companies to more effectively right-size their real estate portfolios. The technology to support on-demand, real time prediction and automatic workspace allocation has arrived.

- **Visitor management**: often aligned to the access and security system, we may choose a separate means of inviting visitors to our workspace that automatically sends directions and potentially a token or QR code that enables them to enter part or all our workspace and notify the host of their arrival.

- **Networking**: often workspace-independent, these apps connect people in a locality, potentially with common interests.

Workspace technology needs to support our strategy – the technology itself isn't the strategy. We don't choose a technology and build everything around it, as it'll evolve far more quickly than our workspace.

Selecting workspace technology therefore presents something of a conundrum. We often want to make sure we invest in the very latest technology, which means waiting until we're close to completing our new workspace. Unless it involves buying hardware, in the main this is possible with subscription-based apps ('software as a service' or SaaS). However, we also want to make sure that our technology isn't just a bolt-on at the end, which requires an early idea of how we want technology to support our strategy.

Selecting technology can therefore differ from the procurement of most services and installations for our new workspace. It requires an early understanding of the range and availability of technology, and an active watching brief until arriving at the latest possible moment to commit safely and practically.

We've covered the key features of our workspace. Drawing on our universal design principles, we'll now consider how we can ensure our workspace considers:

- Inclusivity
- Environmental sustainability
- Wellbeing.

HOW DO WE MAKE OUR WORKSPACE INCLUSIVE?

We want to ensure we create the best possible experience for the way our colleagues are or choose to be. No-one wants to be a 'special case' and to have to raise and issue with the workspace – everyone should be able to use it as comfortably and effectively as the next colleague.

There are several key areas we can focus on to ensure we achieve this aim. We need to think through what we're considering providing regarding:

- **Access**: everyone must be able to get into the workspace and move around freely. Which means we'll have to consider changes in floor levels, ease of movement for those with a disability, door access, signage and wayfinding, surfaces (contrast for visual impairment and material for wheelchair access, for example) and information. Feature staircases – something of a staple for every workspace on more than one floor over the last decade – look grand and are great for many people, but they're immediately discriminatory. Access for colleagues with physical disability should be close by, just as visually evident and not thrown in as an afterthought.

- **Worksetting specification**: many worksettings are inherently geared towards male use – even if unconsciously so. As we've referenced, take bar stools at (typical male) standing height tables, long continuous benches at (typical male) height tables.

- **Worksetting arrangement**: visual and aural disturbance, heightened for the neurodiverse, can be alleviated by careful arrangement of worksettings to ensure their uses don't clash when adjacent. This is also referenced below where Wellbeing is considered.

- **Materials and finishes**: related to the above, a natural, calm palette of colours and materials with clear contrasts between surfaces may not make the biggest visual impact but will ensure the widest possible use of the workspace, particularly in areas where high-focus work will be performed. For our neurodivergent colleagues, this consideration can make or break a workspace.

- **Choice**: it's easy for us to think that our new workspace will suit everyone, just because we're excited by it. For example, our much-trumpeted daylight-filled space may be harmful to someone with sensitivity to light. A choice of settings and location in the workspace is necessary, so that it may be exercised without an issue needing to be raised. As we mentioned earlier, no-one wants to feel like a special case.

- **Amenities**: as with worksettings, many amenities typical to workspace are male-oriented, too, such as foosball and pool tables, and computer games rooms. Gyms decked with free weights and multigyms can also be female-unfriendly. Achieving balance in this regard is hard work, as we often have to challenge societal norms and trends, too.

- **Washrooms**: the designation (or not) of washrooms by gender can be an emotive subject that is best resolved through colleague engagement, taking into account local statutory requirements, too.

As a specific inclusivity consideration, we need to make sure our workspace enables and promotes gender equity. There are three additional considerations in this regard to those references above:

- **Rest space**: we covered the requirements of a wellbeing room above. We sometimes struggle to articulate what 'rest' entails but suffice to say there are varying stages of life for women where the ability to quickly get away from the general workspace into a quiet, confidential and non-disturbed space is extremely important.
- **Free sanitaryware** in female-designated washrooms: of a variety of types, with no restrictions on access and usage.
- Proximity of **lockers** to **washrooms**: for various reasons and at particular stages of life – including pregnancy, post pregnancy and menopause – women may need access to personal items (such as a change of clothing) to take to the washrooms. This may mean a journey from the washroom to the locker and back to the washroom, and so immediate adjacency is vital. The path should also be discreet, and not pass a key amenity such as reception.

HOW DO WE MAKE OUR WORKSPACE ENVIRONMENTALLY SUSTAINABLE?

Safeguarding the environment can often seem too daunting a challenge to even begin to make a meaningful contribution. But every contribution matters. It also sends a clear signal of our organisation's commitment if everybody is behaving responsibly.

Here are some of the things we can do to make an environmental contribution in creating our new workspace:

- **Consumption**: we've all at some stage in our life wondered if we could live with less. The answer is usually yes. There's a simple guide we can follow: avoid, re-use, recycle. While the last of these three is often most focussed on, the most helpful strategy is to avoid buying or consuming in the first place. We need to continually ask ourselves with every proposed component of our new workspace – do we really need this?

- **Waste – recycling**: of course, however responsible we are, consumption and waste will be inevitable. Considerations will need to include the physical repositories (which can be complex and problematic – so are worth handling early, particularly as relates to the design of kitchen and resource areas) and the journey the waste will take. In a shared building the landlord will determine the requirements for segregation. They can include:
  - o Paper
  - o Confidential paper
  - o Food and organic matter
  - o Glass
  - o Plastic
  - o Metal
  - o Electrical
  - o General waste: anything else, or items that contain several materials that cannot be separated.
- **Waste – space**: we often think of waste in tangible terms, as 'things', but empty or under-used workspace is very much a post-pandemic problem, as we're heating, cooling, lighting and servicing it. Whether that's Monday and Friday or the rest of the week, too, the need to right-size our workspace and encourage as much beneficial use as possible, as we covered in Part I, is vital.
- **Sourcing**: supply chains can be long and complex. What we're buying may have its origins in several places. Yet we need to do our very best to prove ethical and sustainable practices and materials throughout. The right questions will need to be asked of suppliers. Those we buy from should be able to tell the full story of the origin of their products.
- **Materiality**: workspace materials and installations such as paint, adhesives and fabrics can contain volatile organic compounds (VOCs), carbon-based substances that evaporate at room temperature. In the short term they can cause headaches, dizziness and nausea, and long-term far more serious conditions. We need to make sure all materials selected are free of VOCs.
- **Energy use**: even in shared buildings, energy usage is often separately metred by tenant and so efficiencies and reduction

can be targeted and tracked. It often means more hardware such as sensors, but in most cases with a clear payback.

- **Accreditation**: environmental performance is often understood in terms of the certificates hanging on the wall. They're worth pursuing, for what they require, what they say and the ability to compare with others. But a degree of caution is required. Obtaining a certificate doesn't always mean our job is done. The requirements aren't necessarily our priorities, and when complete we may not even understand what we've done as the process was managed on our behalf.

HOW DO WE CREATE A WORKSPACE FOCUSSED ON WELLBEING?

Another of our six 'universal principles' is wellbeing. Our workspace is for human habitation, and so the needs – conscious and unconscious; physical, mental and emotional – of humans should be at its heart.

There are several things we can do to contribute to the wellbeing of our colleagues in our workspace, some of which are covered elsewhere in Part II:

- **Air** quality: to ensure adequate fresh, filtered air, with the minimisation of the presence of carbon dioxide (CO_2) levels as the undue presence of CO_2 is proven to negatively affect concentration levels.
- Control over **light** levels (too little or too much), from two sources:
  - **External**: the passage of the **sun** around our workspace must be understood before the design of our workspace begins. Ideally we want direct sunlight in our social zones, but not where we may have focussed or desk space. Or we'll have great light and views but the internal blinds down all day. This degree of planning lessens the need for some of the suggestions below.
  - **Internal**: where ceiling-mounted light levels are low this may require local task lighting, and where glare from the sun is likely to impact the workspace, local, adjustable blinds.

- A **choice** of worksettings for all the activities typically undertaken in a day; and just as importantly permission to exercise the choice.
- The effective **arrangement** of worksettings that positions settings for focussed activity away from main thoroughfares and social spaces and breaks up open space with visual dividers (e.g. storage, shelves, plants and furniture).
- Control over **noise** levels and the potential for **disturbance**: sensitivity to types and volume of noise can particularly impact those who are neurodiverse, even to the extent of rendering the workspace impossible to work in. Which means we need to consider:
  - The provision of **focus areas** away from collaborative and social areas where the clear signal (potentially with an actual sign) is 'do not disturb'.
  - A balance of hard and soft **surfaces** and materials throughout the workspace.
  - Feature **acoustic panels** or sound absorbing surfaces (such as cork) on walls in both open space and enclosed rooms.
  - Suitable **spacing** of adjacent desks or, preferably, some form of sound absorbent barrier between them to help them be used simultaneously.
  - A **sound masking** system ('white noise') – this may be mechanical, mimicking the sound of a building ventilation system, or be ambient sounds or music.
- **Rest** or **quiet** spaces: away from the main workspace. This is in addition to the **wellbeing room** referenced earlier in Part II.
- **Refresh** facilities: water and tea/coffee points, refrigerators and food preparation surfaces with sufficient space to eat and drink.
- **Control** over the working environment – temperature, humidity and lighting, in particular. This isn't always directly possible in a shared building where the plant and systems are controlled by the landlord's team, but there should be as a minimum the means to request changes as required.
- A focus on **comfort** and **ergonomics** in all worksettings and amenities, as referenced earlier in Part II.

- Facilities for **cyclists**, runners and walkers: storage areas, drying facilities and female, male and gender-neutral showers and lockers.
- Internal **planting**: as mentioned in Part II – both for oxygen generation and CO_2 removal, and to create a beneficial sense of connection with the outdoors.
- A simple, easy and discreet means of **getting help** or making wellbeing-related requests. Our needs will change over time.

It's worth noting that there are many other factors contributing to the wellbeing of our colleagues that the workspace can't influence that will ideally need to be considered. In additional to those covered in the earlier chapter on workplace experience are:

- Management philosophy
- Management practice – the example set by senior leaders
- Job role design
- Work/personal life boundaries
- Opportunities to safely raise difficult matters
- 'Speak out' schemes with guaranteed anonymity.

As mentioned earlier – but worth re-stating – a fantastic workspace won't fix a toxic culture.

HOW DO WE MAKE OUR WORKSPACE 'DOG FRIENDLY'?

The presence of pets – by which we usually mean dogs (rather than bird-eating spiders) – in the workspace often divides opinion, sometimes passionately. To this extent, in respect of our colleague population, they're a niche interest and therefore it can be argued that allowing dogs reduces the inclusivity of our workspace.

There are many advantages of allowing dogs in the workspace some or all the time. Dogs can:

- **Reduce stress** and anxiety – interacting with dogs can release endorphins and lower blood pressure.
- Boost **happiness** and positivity, and therefore (potentially) productivity.

- Encourage colleagues to take **breaks** (hopefully not to clear up a mess!).
- Improve staff **attraction** and retention.
- In the hybrid working era, prompt higher levels of workspace **attendance**, as colleagues don't have to stay home to look after their dog(s).
- Boost the organisation's **brand** and image, showing it to be a caring and responsible.

TRUE STORY

In the wake of Covid-19, a digital content company grappled with the unexpected 'pandemic puppy surge'. Employees had adopted dogs during lockdown, not quite realising the full extent of their return-to-office schedules. Leaders, keen to accommodate both four-legged friends and their human counterparts, had to think on their paws. The compromise was simple yet effective: designate 'dog days' twice a week, creating specific zones for those with canine companions, while respecting the space of those with allergies or canine-related concerns. Another company navigated lease restrictions with an annual 'paws in work' day for a spot of stress relief, and a dog food company, with a more naturally pet-friendly ethos, welcomed dogs any day, no questions asked. Introducing dogs into the workplace isn't without its hairy moments, but with thoughtful planning, it's possible to keep both tail-waggers and their human friends content.

Any promises to colleagues of being able to bring dogs to the workspace should be thoroughly considered before being made. The issues we need to be aware of include:

- **Permission**: does the landlord permit dogs? If not, the issue may be a non-starter.
- **Opinion**: do our colleagues have a preference for or against dogs being present? We need to ask. If the view is not unanimously in favour and we accept a majority verdict, we need to be prepared to manage the views of those who objected, as their concerns may be serious.

- **Restrictions**: do we want to always allow dogs or do so on particular days and at designated times? We may also wish to designate physical areas of the workspace as suitable for dogs and include dog-suitable features – which limits the flexibility of our workspace.
- **Behaviour**: not all dogs are adequately trained, or friendly towards people or other dogs. Dogs brought to the workspace must be able to cope with the experience in an appropriately agreeable way, and not add unnecessary disturbance. A little like people!
- **Health** and **safety**: dogs don't use washrooms. There may be hygiene-related issues, that could also impose a burden on our FM team.
- **Facilities** and **amenities**: dogs come with baggage – bowls, food and beds, to name a few items. They create a requirement for hygienic and appropriate storage and may limit the flexibility of our workspace as a result.
- **Policy**: we'll need a clear, unambiguous policy on what's expected of dogs and their owners, with appropriate sanctions where the policy isn't complied with.
- **Liabilities**: 'dog bites man' is news if it happens in the workspace. We'll need to ensure we check and are comfortable with our liabilities to employees and visitors, and the impact on our insurances.

What therefore seems on the face of it a simple 'yes or no' issue can be a complex consideration.

WHAT OTHER THINGS WILL WE NEED TO THINK OF?

We've considered all the worksettings and technology we need, and the look and feel we'd like to achieve; our workspace is being designed and the team is working brilliantly well together. But there's stuff missing.

These are some of what we'll need to consider and plan for – the things that make our workspace 'whole', that finish it. We may need to procure them directly, which means special attention will need to be paid to coordinating our choices with the rest of the project team and ensure that our cost consultant knows what's going on.

- **Branding**: the space needs to feel like it belongs to our organisation so that we, as occupants, feel like we belong to it, too. We need to avoid over-doing it, or 'billboarding' (so it looks like an external advertising hoarding), but it can be done subtly by weaving some of the colours, shades, imagery and symbols of the organisation – but not to the exclusion of all other options. If the brand colour is purple, not everything has to be purple. Better still, the essence of the brand values and attributes can be expressed through materials choice and the tone of voice in messaging.
- **Signage and wayfinding**: depending on the nature of the space and architecture, colleagues and visitors may need help to find their way. This also needs to link to the brand and the design of the workspace itself. If a specialist signage firm is engaged, they should work closely with our interior architect, too. The complexity of this exercise shouldn't be underestimated, so sufficient time should be made available to decide on style and content. The types of signage include:
  - o Statutory: fire and safety signage, made in a legally prescribed format, installed by the general contractor as part of the fit-out.
  - o Wayfinding: directions and zoning.
  - o Information: labelling on doors and cupboards, for example.
  - o Temporary: for the facilities management team to use where, for example, equipment malfunctions or spaces need cleaning.
  - o Manifestation: treatment to glazing to both alert to it being present, obscure content or occupants in meeting rooms and prevent AV camera tracking.
- **Planting**: it's been realised in workspace design in the last decade or so something that has been instinctively known for millennia – that as humans, we like being close to nature. Live plants add colour, texture, oxygen and delight to any

workspace. We'll need to be aware that they may also add small bugs, which like to live on plants. At a high level there's no harm in adding artificial or 'petrified' (once living, now 'frozen') planting to complement the effect of live installations.

- **Coffee machines**: while not everyone drinks coffee, the term 'coffee' means both the drink itself and the cafe experience. It can be both a 'fast lane' (push-button) and a 'slow lane' (traditional barista-style) offer. But where coffee is provided it should be of the highest quality possible, to match what the high street offers. Which means ensuring the machine is bean-to-cup and has fresh milk, too.
- **Filtered water**: along with coffee, filtered still and sparkling water is now an expectation in a workspace. Systems that provide it also ensure crates of single-use plastic bottles won't be necessary, so plastic cups should be avoided, too. Re-usable metal bottles issued as a welcome give-away are usually the best route (as long as colleagues take the time to wash them!).

To name or number?

A special mention is needed here for room and worksetting naming and numbering to aid wayfinding. It can become an involved and sometimes emotive part of the project, particularly as it relates to meeting rooms.

A common complaint in workspaces is that meeting rooms are hard to find. A name doesn't tell you where a room is unless a clever coding system is used. Yet a number is fairly dull and has no brand resonance. So, the recommended approach is to use both – an underlying number that says which floor, wing or zone the room is in, with a sequential number, and then a name if required 'on top' that.

We may also wish to include a learning element in room naming, where perhaps people's names or particular ideas or places are used, with information available outside or in the room.

TRUE STORY

In response to a present workspace in which no-one could find meeting rooms, wasting considerable colleague time and causing a lot of frustration, one of the authors created a meeting room numbering scheme for a new workspace that divided the rectangular space into north, south, east and west to aid orientation. Every room was given a number as building, floor, zone (NSEW) and sequential number. It seemed helpful and logical. But it was wholly rejected by the occupants, to much amusement from the author's colleagues. Sometimes we try too hard and should test our ideas with occupants of the space before we implement them, better still, involve our colleagues in the naming process. To avoid embarrassment if nothing else.

HOW DO WE MAKE SURE OUR WORKSPACE PROJECT STAYS ON BUDGET?

By the concept design stage, our cost consultant will turn our budget into a cost plan. They'll know exactly what to price, down to individual items and finishes, using their knowledge of market prices.

It's often the case that our grand ambitions approved by our SteerCo, when translated into workspace design, can't all be afforded and that some educated choices will be required. It's unlikely in post-pandemic markets, that the mere act of tendering construction will deliver the savings sought as perhaps it once did.

So, we'll likely need to reduce our costs. The process is often called **value engineering** (VE) which is a posh (and less scary) term for cutting costs. There are two approaches:

1   Removing **specific features**, whether amenities (such as a gym or exercise room), worksettings (often those at the more 'relaxed' end of the spectrum) or support spaces (such as a

dedicated IT support area) from the workspace. This can be obvious and, as a result, disappointing. Unless it's the slide, which will come as a blessed relief; or

2   Shaving **layers** of cost from the overall workspace, maintaining the design integrity and balance of worksettings and amenities, through:

a. Reducing quantities.
b. Substituting materials and finishes for lower cost alternatives.
c. Buying standard 'off the shelf' items instead of having them made specially (a typical approach being to buy furniture items instead of having things made in a joinery mill).

It's possible that several rounds of VE will be required to bring the scheme within the Cost plan. That is, without eating into our contingency at this stage, as this will be required to meet typical design coordination and construction matters that invariably arise during a project.

Too long spent on VE, however, will impact the project programme, which will in turn have a cost impact. VE therefore must be conducted efficiently and quickly, as there will be SteerCo approval to obtain, too, and potentially even re-work should SteerCo not approve it first time around.

When we've got our design scheme within the cost plan, we're ready to crack on and build it.

THINGS TO LOOK OUT FOR

Here's some things to look out for in this area, to challenge or avoid:

• **'We want a workspace where people leave feeling better than when they arrived.'** While making our workspace healthy and habitable should always be foremost in our minds, caution is needed over some claims of the potential regenerative power our workspace. There are simply too many other influences on our wellbeing to separate its contribution. Our role is to do best for our colleagues in this regard.

- **'We need a palette of worksettings to reflect everything we do in a day.'** Which would be fine were it not for having to battle the temptation to respond to minor differences in the type of meeting we have, for example, with a setting to suit each. This level of complexity will needlessly and understandably confuse our colleagues. We're adaptable creatures. We can also smell BS a mile off.

- **'Our workspace needs to be Instagram-ready.'** We live in a world of instant appraisal, in which 'cool' has a continuing allure. Our workspace will be photographed and shared immediately it's seen. Even if we're taking our colleagues on a tour while it's being built. But while the aesthetic is incredibly important, the workspace must work. Taking pictures of something working as intended is tricky. The battle between function and form has been raging for thousands of years, yet they're on the same side if we want them to be. On occasions cool has to submit to functionality. But as always, it's about balance. Fundamentally, our workspace must be people, organisation and planet ready.

- **'A fantastic workspace will create the right culture.'** The potential cultural impact of new workspace mustn't be over-promised, it won't transform an entire workplace culture. We must work with what we have and do what we can. The process of creating a new workspace may itself tell us a great deal about the openness or competence of leadership, and what else might ned to change to create a positive cultural impact.

- **Pointless is worse than basic**. If something is mandated or included that is simply a gesture or is covering up a misgiving, our colleagues will see it from a distance and will run the other way.

We're now ready to build and operate our new workspace.

PART III

HOW DO WE MAKE OUR WORKSPACE HAPPEN?

7

DELIVER
HOW WILL WE BUILD OUR WORKSPACE?

During this stage of project, we're going to build our space, furnish it, decide how we're going to – use it day-to-day, get ready to move and make absolutely sure we think of everything (and even if we don't, we'll be prepared to deal with the unexpected)!

HOW DO WE BUY CONSTRUCTION?

We're ready to buy and build our workspace scheme.

It's worth saying at this stage that we'll be helped considerably with this task by our project manager and/or cost consultant. We'll need to be aware of what's needed and how it happens, along with engaging our internal legal and finance colleagues, but we won't be expected to run this tender ourselves.

In Part II we considered a choice of two broad approaches to procuring construction to help us bring on board the right professional team – design and build (D&B) and traditional. We'll say more about them here. A reminder – neither approach guarantees a better outcome, it's all down to how we manage the project and the decisions we take.

DOI: 10.4324/9781003442684-10

All construction contracts will normally comprise four elements:

1 **Construction management**. This will comprise a small team directly employed by the general contractor.
2 **Trade packages**: the actual construction works, broken down by specialist trade or profession.
3 **Preliminaries** (often shortened to simply 'prelims'): the items that are necessary to allow the general contractor to carry out the works but don't comprise any of the trade packages. They include things like site accommodation, procurement services, statutory approvals and insurances.
4 General contractor **overheads and profit** (sometimes shortened to 'OHP').

Under both approaches, we'll have two key responsibilities:

- We'll need to appoint a **contract administrator** to represent our organisation regarding all the formalities agreed within the contract. This is usually either our cost consultant or project manager, but there will likely be a separate fee for this from whoever takes it on.
- Payments will be **staged** monthly throughout the contract. As the general contractor must pay their trade subcontractors, payment terms are often requested to be reduced from an organisation's standard terms, sometimes to as short as 7–14 days. Each month, our contract administrator will work closely with the general contractor to 'value' the work undertaken during the period and issue a Certificate to this effect to accompany an invoice.

Our finance team will need to be made aware of how payments will be requested from suppliers and contractors, so they can put the necessary process in place. It's worth noting that the costs of the general contractor stopping work due to non-payment can be significant, so we need to avoid the possibility.

For the duration of the construction contract, our workspace will be under the direct control of the general contractor, and we won't have any rights of access without following the general contractor's security and safety procedures. This means we'll have to seek permission whenever we want to visit the site, and to wear **personal protective equipment** (PPE) while on site, usually termed '5-point' – hard hat, safety boots, high-visibility jacket, safety gloves and safety glasses. There should be sufficient sets provided for visitors as part of the contract.

We'll need to be always escorted on site by one of the construction team; for those unfamiliar with a construction site, hazards lurk everywhere.

Design and build: specifics

If we decided on the design and build (D&B) route, we'll already be committed to working with a single construction firm. There are two approaches to costing within D&B that we need to be aware of:

- **Lump sum**: during the design process, as progressively more is known about what will be created, a final fixed lump sum will be presented that includes everything other than client-direct items and services. This approach has the advantage of providing cost certainty, but there's unlikely to be a great deal of transparency. That is, if we want to know how much decoration is costing, (for example), it won't be declared. We will need to ask to see the lump sum broken down into its various trades.
- **Open book**: where some or all of the 'line item' (trade) 'package' costs will be visible, along with tendered costs (usually from three subcontractors), with a statement of the general contractor's preliminaries, overheads and profit.

Traditional: specifics

Where the Traditional route is chosen, it'll be on an open book basis. The entire design scheme will need to be offered to the market in a competitive tender. This will be led by our cost consultant and project manager.

At the time of the tender, due to time constraints, design will not usually be 100% complete and specified. Our interior architect will instead specify the type of installation and performance levels required of particular elements, and the general contractor will be asked to finish the design, specify the product and obtain the price. Our interior architect might state, for example, glazed doors with matt black powder coated frames with a 35dB sound rating. The general contractor will find a suitable product that meets the requirements and submit to the interior architect for approval.

It's usual to ask the bidding contractors to recommend further value engineering (VE – as described in Part II) at the tender stage.

A period of a month is typically allowed for tenders for construction to be submitted. Our cost consultant and project manager will receive, analyse and report on the tenders, with a recommendation. We'll need to meet the bidding firms and be satisfied with their approach and their proposed on-site construction manager.

When we're ready to commit, depending on the country in which the work is taking place, there are usually standard forms of contract. Our legal team will need to be involved to satisfy themselves the contract is in order, and insurances are in place together with (importantly) all health and safety processes.

HOW DO WE BUY FURNITURE?

A whole book could probably be written about how to buy workspace furniture – a summary is provided here.

Unlike buying construction services, buying furniture will likely involve a tender that we'll need to run and manage. While some D&B firms offer 'full turnkey solutions', and through the traditional method we'll be assisted in buying furniture by our interior architect, project manager and cost consultant, it's advisable for us to take an active role get the result we want.

Re-use

As mentioned in Part I, our first task is to audit what we have and agree what we're going to **re-use**. In doing so, the time, logistics and costs we'll need to consider include:

- **Dismantling** – note the risk of breakage or the product not going back together properly again (some furniture is designed to be assembled and sited once only).
- **Transporting** and potentially **storing** for a period. We can't make assumptions of being able to store anything on the construction site.
- **Delivering** and **re-assembling** (with the hope that all the component parts remain intact and can be located).

When considering items for re-use, we should work with our interior architect to look beneath the surface. Items may appear to be at the end of their life, but we can repair or replace component parts, while re-using the parts still functioning and in good condition. Chairs can be re-upholstered and seat pads replaced, table and desktops replaced, for example.

While it's important to strive to re-use as much as possible for sustainability reasons, it can sometimes be more expensive to achieve than to buy new – which, for so many reasons, seems wrong. It's a decision our SteerCo will need to make. Which is also why, where new is chosen, seeking out sustainable suppliers is so important.

Scheduling and tendering

Thereafter, our interior architect – or furniture consultant if we appointed one – will prepare a **schedule** of new furniture required, including make, model, price, quantity and total, usually with a picture. The schedule will be taken off, and hence reconcile to, the final layout plans, hence the expression 'take-offs'. Schedules are cumbersome and impractical beasts when created in Excel, but ideally that's the format we want it in. The schedule will combine **systems** (desks of all types and 'task' – or ergonomic – seating) and **loose** furniture (everything else).

Our schedule should also contain details of all re-used items, to be noted as such. This helps with ensuring that we have a complete and accurate inventory of all furniture requirements against our layout plans.

A fun part of any workspace project is the **showroom tour**. Manufacturers are often clustered in the same area in major cities, and so taking an interested party of colleagues to see and try furniture is a useful and engaging part of the tender process.

As mentioned earlier, furniture manufacturers rarely, if ever, sell directly to workspace residents, so we'll need to manage a tender exercise, whereby **furniture dealers** will be asked to submit costs for the products, storage, delivery and project management. Appropriate dealers can be recommended by our interior architect or project manager. The benefits of using dealers, both for clients and manufacturers, are:

- **Ease**: the furniture order (known as a 'schedule') could comprise products from 20–30 different manufacturers – possibly even up to 50–60.
- **Responsibility**: a single point of contact and contract if anything goes awry or amiss.
- **Experience**: it's their core business; they'll get the best deals and take the hassle off our hands.

The furniture schedule will often include 'named' products, (made by furniture manufacturers that are well-known in the industry), which means that the dealers will all be going to the same manufacturers to obtain prices. Some dealers will be approved or licensed dealers for some of the manufacturers, and so will get preferential pricing, others won't. The tender should offer dealers a chance to recommend **substitutions** where they may be able to achieve the same style as that proposed, but at a lower price or improved sustainability rating.

Commercial or 'contract' furniture **pricing** works on high list prices and large discounts – which can be up to 60–70%. The items are rarely stocked, and so lead times for most items are a minimum of around 4–6 weeks for systems furniture, and for loose items, it can be anything up to 12–16 weeks. Lead times in some parts of the world can be impacted by summer factory shutdowns, increasing these times by 2–4 weeks.

Considerations other than price with our schedule will include:

- **Supply chain**: including responsible sourcing and ethical practices.
- **Sustainability**: materials, manufacturing and assembly processes, and end-of-life intent.

- **Warranties**: which for most products should be 5–10 years.
- **Continuity** of supply and maintenance: often guaranteed where required.

The dealer should be able to detail each for the products scheduled.

Finally, it's always a good idea to order a small surplus of the most-used items, in particular desk chairs (or 'task' as they are known) and meeting chairs, to keep as spares, or **attic stock**. While faulty chairs will be replaced by the supplier, the lead time on replacements could leave our colleagues short of seating.

Cable management

A fully functional desk contains a complex mix of IT and electrical kit. The desk itself – the slab of wood with four legs and a cable tray – is the easy part.

IT and related kit usually include:

- Monitor(s)
- Monitor arms
- USB docking station – which may be integrated with the monitor
- Desktop power/USB charging module
- Keyboard
- Mouse
- All necessary connecting cables.

IT kit generally isn't especially beautiful – monitors are usually black or dark grey, monitor arms are functional beasts, twin monitors often end up at different heights and angles, and keyboards and mice can be strewn all over the surface.

Cables especially aren't pretty. There are two cabling issues to be concerned about:

- From the building's **floor slab** to the **desk**. Cables will either come up through grommets in the raised access floor and terminate in power and data 'blocks' in the cable tray or will terminate at a floor box set into the raised access floor (if there is one) and be connected into the desk from there. Either way, there will be cables coming from the floor to the desk. They'll need to come up through the desk leg or a cable 'sock' or 'umbilical', to avoid dangling exposed. Note that raised access floors are not common in all countries, and in those where they are typically found, may not be possible to fit in older buildings. In such cases, a combination of ceiling-distributed and surface mounted cable runs (which can often be made into a design feature) will be required, along with the careful positioning of desks and other worksettings next to walls and columns.

- From the connections in the **cable tray** to the **equipment**. It's preferable to have as much kit set into the cable tray of the desk as possible to avoid it being on display and subject to being tampered with. This also ensures a tidier presentation on the desk surface.

It's a good idea to draw a diagram that shows who will be providing and installing each component. This means working with our IT team and the general contractor. We may have to be the ones to do this.

Height adjustable desks have two cable trays, just to complicate matters. A different diagram will be needed for these.

Similar diagrams will be needed in all meeting rooms and spaces where there's audio visual or presentation kit, too. There, 'power boxes' within tables will need to be specified, usually set below the surface of the table and accessed via a flap, containing power and data cables and outlets, along with screen connectivity if required.

As referenced when we covered technology (it's worth stating twice), as many worksettings as possible should provide power; it can be the difference between a worksetting being used or not. Despite advances in mobile connectivity, unfortunately 'battery anxiety' is still very much a thing!

Payment terms

As covered, construction operates on payment terms that may be unfamiliar to our organisation – so too does furniture. But they are different again.

It varies by country and supplier, but it's likely that a deposit will be due on placement of order, of up to 50% of the total value, on a pro-forma invoice. The order usually won't be processed until the money is received. This is because almost all the products in the schedule will be made to order. Further staged payments will be due on delivery (say 30%) and again on completion (the remaining 20%). It's therefore worth priming our finance colleagues in advance.

Delivery and installation

Even on small contracts, furniture installation may take up to 2 weeks. There will need to be agreement with the general contractor if furniture is to be installed prior to practical completion, (PC). This means that deliveries and access will be the responsibility of the general contractor. Very often, pressure on the programme for completion will require that furniture is installed prior to PC. A clean site is desirable at this stage, a requirement usually understood by a general contractor.

While there's a risk of damaging the items being installed as some construction works may be finishing, as well as damage to constructed features (usually walls and doors) in the process of furniture installation, co-ordination with the appropriate trades such as electrical and IT installers may be required during the installation.

SHOULD WE BUILD A PILOT SPACE?

Before we buy construction and furniture, it's worth considering creating a slice of the new workspace in the existing workspace. It could be in an area that's presently unused, or an area could be cleared for the purpose. This is termed a **pilot** space.

A clarification is necessary between a pilot and an experiment:

- An **experiment** occurs early in a design process, usually to prove (or not) an idea or hunch, with a potential for many outcomes. We've moved way beyond this stage for our workspace overall, albeit some worksettings, furniture or technology may be considered experimental.
- A **pilot** is a test of a product or service close to completion, to refine the detail and obtain initial user feedback. It's rarely, if ever, the basis for a 'go/no-go' decision.

A pilot space is a fantastic engagement opportunity for our colleagues, as well as a valuable source of reaction and insight. It's generally a good idea if we're undergoing a longer-term construction project, so people can see intended changes, learn new behaviours and adapt *before* the real deal is done. Depending on the budget we may include carpets or other flooring, wall finishes, lighting, furniture and desktop IT. It creates an ideal opportunity to test the desk cabling with the full IT set-up.

TRUE STORY

An organisation was moving several thousand people to a radical new workspace in a brand-new building under construction, and wanted to make sure all colleagues experienced it in advance. They created a pilot space in their existing building for the purpose. They planned for several hundred colleagues at a time to spend two months in the pilot space over a period of two years. The first two groups loved the space so much they were aghast at having to return to their existing workspace for the next couple of years and expressed a preference to stay in the new space. Change journeys can be long, and what looks like a logical approach in planning can sometimes provoke an understandably emotional reaction. Considering our plan from our colleagues' perspective is vital.

A pilot space also gives us the opportunity to create a 'Change HQ' for the project through to completion, where we might hold events and make information available.

HOW ARE WE GOING TO USE OUR WORKSPACE?

How we're going to use the workspace is an area in which our colleagues will be keenly interested, as they'll have their own preferences.

The benefit of designing in flexibility is that, even from initial consultation to move-in day, things (both internally and externally) can and will change. So, it's important to know we have several options for planning worksetting use:

- **Allocated**: individuals are assigned a worksetting – usually a desk – on a 1:1 basis. While this often satisfies the individuals, it's highly inflexible and takes considerable time to manage and maintain. It can also lead to under-utilisation given variable patterns of attendance, and therefore high per-person costs.
- **Team zones**: teams are designated a specific zone, usually consistent with an overall ratio of people to worksettings. While this provides certainty for teams, unless the zones are very loose it can require regular re-planning of the workspace as team composition and relationships evolve.
- **Free address**: anyone can sit anywhere they like at any time. While this is highly flexible and requires minimal management, teams often struggle to co-locate when they need, and so a 'home-made' team zone allocation usually results, where teams themselves determine their preferred location – with which there's nothing wrong at all. Free address doesn't stay free for very long. It's also a strategy that requires very little stored or bespoke material, or a central store area that does not root a team in a particular part of the workspace.
- **Mixed**: a combination of the above, given the differing nature of our teams and some individuals, can ensure we account for all needs. It can however be perceived as a first and second class offer and require considerable management time, not least in resolving disputes. As referenced earlier, while one size certainly doesn't fit all, one super-flexible size can fit most.

The above are all independent of any technology that may be deemed necessary. Space scheduling, desk booking and collaboration tools can all be used with all approaches except the first, where they won't be necessary. It's vital, however that the usage approach is agreed – at least in principle – **before** the technology is sourced.

The workspace usage strategy that's put in place for day one isn't a one-off decision. As with many aspects of the workspace in use, it can be modified if the opening approach isn't proving to be partially or wholly workable. It's important to ensure colleagues are aware of this through our communication, to allay any initial concerns.

HOW WILL WE MANAGE THE MOVE?

As noted in Part II, our move may be one of the following:

- Within the same space, progressively making space for renovation work.
- Out of our existing space, either to another space or remote, and back in full when the renovation is complete.
- To a new workspace.

Essentially the same process is required.

Getting organised

As the move will be a client direct service, as project leader we're going to be heavily involved. We'll need help both internally and externally:

- Internally: **move coordinators**. They'll work closely with the change champions for their team, as we covered in Part II. They're usually administrators within teams, where everyone will need someone responsible for:
  - o Validating the master list of colleagues moving (see below).
  - o Ensuring everyone in their team is accounted for.
  - o Ensuring the clear-outs of the old workspace happen effectively.
  - o Identifying special needs and communicating them to the project team (as there may be design implications).
  - o Looking after the needs of those who'll be absent during the move out, move back (if it's the existing workspace being renovated) or move to the new workspace.
  - o In the new workspace, unpacking and returning crates to the move contractors.
- Externally: **move managers** and **move contractors**. They're not the same (a distinction that's easy to miss):
  - o **Move managers**: will take full responsibility for organising the move, tendering move contractors, ensuring everything ends up where it should do, and that our present location is entirely clear when we leave.

- **Move contractors**: the people who move our stuff, with labour, crates and vehicles. They're almost always the people who also dismantle, move and re-assemble our IT kit, under the guidance of our IT project lead.

We'll have to decide whether we're happy acting as the move manager or not, based on time, cost and capability considerations. Albeit we may not have a choice!

Who, what, how and where

We'll need two key information registers:

- A **master list** of all our people moving. This will be useful not just for the move but for creating distribution lists, too. Sometimes in move terms it's called a **move matrix**. It should include their name, role title, department or team, e-mail address and where they're moving from (building and floor). If our new workspace is to be allocated, it'll also need to include where they're moving to. Data privacy issues may require this to be shared between a restricted number of people in a secure online location.
- **Kit inventories** of all items that are moving. After a decade or more pre-pandemic of the trend being towards creating brand new, fully equipped 'ready to use' workspace, meaning a very light move, the re-use of furniture and IT kit has meant a trend towards larger moves once again. Albeit with less paper. We'll need this split between:
  - **Furniture**: which we'll have identified when buying furniture, so should already be to hand.
  - **IT**: where if we're confident we have enough of everything, we may not specifically list but will just make sure is organised as we depart.

Clearing out our stuff

Despite the pandemic lessening our dependence on stored material, right down to many colleagues now not even needing a locker (covered below), a clear-out will still be needed. Probably several as we rarely make a decision on everything in one go, which means the first must happen as early as possible. Options for where our stuff will go include:

- **The bin**. Simple as that. Hopefully the recycle bin. Which means more need to be provided.
- **Archive**: but only if it's vitally important or we're legally required to retain it. Archives aren't there to store what we don't know what to do with.
- **Digitisation** and then either the bin or archive.
- **Home**: if it's our stuff – but we shouldn't store business materials at home.

The complexity of the physical move will very much depend on:

- The state we're presently in. If we used the pandemic to migrate to being a **digital first** organisation, it'll likely be easy. That means, the digital origination, distribution, storage of and access to information. If we didn't, and our workspace is stacked with paper and 'stuff' to which we keep adding, it may be trickier, and we'll need to start the big cleanse earlier.
- Whether we're creating our new workspace in the same space as our existing, requiring that we clear out for a period before moving back, or we're moving to a new location.
- Whether we're without a workspace between leaving our present workspace and occupying our new, or moving straight in.

The key challenge with our colleagues will be conveying the allowance for storage of business and personal items in our new workspace and how this relates to move crates.

Clearing out our furniture and IT

While we're probably targeting the re-use of furniture, desktop and AV IT kit, it's unlikely we'll be moving everything. So, we'll need a plan for the balance.

IT kit is usually cleared in one or more of four possible ways:

- Re-used at other locations (if we have them).
- Staff sale or giveaway: albeit it's likely what's left won't be especially desirable at home. If it is, logistically it's a straightforward process.
- Charitable or 'good cause' donation, such as schools or youth clubs: albeit for the same reason as the above, it might not be wanted.
- Sustainably disposed of by a specialist firm, with none of the components going to landfill. Very often our move contractors can handle this on our behalf.

Furniture is a little more problematic. It's far bulkier, often requires dismantling, and other than for licensed pieces, is often worth very little the moment it's unwrapped from new. Our possible disposal routes are like the above, but often prove trickier than with IT kit.

Charities and good cause destinations often have specific needs requiring space planning in addition to dismantling, transport and re-assembly tasks and costs. Staff sales can be logistically impractical and difficult to administer. Both require considerable time to manage. Noble aims therefore often get overtaken by other project priorities. Success relies on starting as early as possible with planning and communication and dedicating a person to managing it separate from the project team.

Moving out and in

Four key tasks during moving out and in that we must be aware of (and our move managers will handle, if we've appointed them) are:

- Understanding our responsibilities for **site clearance**, in detail. It usually entails removing everything that – if the building were turned upside down and shaken – would fall out. So, stuff that's fixed to walls and floors wouldn't need to be cleared. Formally checking with the landlord well in advance is advised.
- Liaison with building management at each end, to ensure **vehicle access** on the days required and any special loading bay requirements, together with goods lift access noting any weight or size restrictions.

- Where required, providing **security** for the move at either or both ends.
- Where required, ensuring a **lift engineer** is available at either or both ends. The whole scheduled activity can be derailed if a goods lift fails and there's no-one on hand to repair it immediately.

HOW DO WE PLAN FOR LOCKERS?

It was common in the days where every desk was individually assigned to find pedestals (usually a set of lockable drawers on wheels) under each one. With the move to more flexible workspaces with a range of shared worksettings, the provision of under-desk personal storage space moved to banks of lockers, usually found grouped together and distributed around the workspace. The subject of lockers can be unexpectedly complex, so warrant inclusion in this guide!

It should be noted that lockers must be included as part of the workspace design, not a last-minute add-in. They can be an engaging feature and be used for sub-dividing space. The back of lockers can also be useful as a collaborative space work wall.

Providing lockers means that several choices need to be made:

- Will we **re-use** some or all our existing lockers, if we have them (in which case they'll probably need to be re-numbered)?
- If we need new, will they be a **furniture** item (standard) or **joinery** (bespoke)?
- What **size**? It's always advisable not to scrimp on capacity – enough for a day bag or rucksack, papers, a laptop and several pairs of shoes. Although too big and we'll end up being able to fit a kitchen sink.
- Will they be **uniform**? They don't all have to be the same; they can consider different colleague needs. But this adds planning and management complexity.
- What **locking** mechanism? There are usually three choices – key, punch-code or software app.
- How many **units high**? They can take up a lot of floorspace, so the tendency is to stack them as high as possible – even up

to five units. Beware – this means that only tall people can be allocated the top row.

That's just the hardware. Then decisions need to be made over their allocation and use:

- Who **gets** one? Everyone – or just those who request them? Or no-one, such that they're all 'day lockers?' In the hybrid working era, demand for lockers is declining as people have got used to only bringing what they need into the workspace for the day.
- How will they be **numbered**? Or named? Or identified – say with magnets or photos?
- How will lockers that are **no longer used** or needed be managed?
- What **permission** will colleagues have to give for their locker to be opened if it's deemed a prohibited item is being stored in it? This may include food, illegal substances or stolen items.

It's often the case, too, that the common areas of a shared building will include lockers for clothes, the rules for the use of which will be determined by the building management team.

We'll need to include guidance on the provision and management of lockers for both our workspace and the common areas in our workplace guide, also covered in this part of the book.

HOW DO WE CONTROL CHANGES DURING CONSTRUCTION?

'Change control' (concerning 'things') isn't the same as change management (all about people). However fixed we believe our design to be at the point construction begins, it rarely is – we'll change our minds, or something will emerge that either isn't as we thought it would be or that has had an unexpected effect.

We therefore need a rigorous process for understanding, managing and progressing changes while the construction team is on site. Changes impact cost, programme and sometimes other areas of the workspace.

Change control will be managed by our contract administrator, and will cover:

- **Desirability**: do we really need this change? Or is it cosmetic? It's quite likely it'll only be confirmed as needed when the cost and programme impact are known, so an early estimate of each will be needed.
- **Feasibility**: can it be accommodated? True story: one of the authors witnessed during a project meeting on site a discussion to explore whether a lift core could be relocated.
- Effects on **other things**: our interior architect and M&E designer will need to confirm whether anything else is impacted by the change.
- **Programme**: the full impact on programme of the change will need to be assessed – which will potentially affect cost.
- **Cost**: the total cost of the change will need to be calculated.
- **Approval**: the change will need to be formally accepted by us and incorporated into the construction programme and cost plan.
- **Confirmation**: the change will need to be notified to all interested parties.

HOW DO WE MAKE SURE WE THINK OF EVERYTHING?

Some refer to the process of easing out of the construction phase and getting ourselves into a position to welcome our colleagues to their new workspace as **soft landings**. That's to underestimate just how much there is to think of and do. There's nothing 'soft' about it, it's hard work; sometimes it feels like we're landing a light aircraft in high cross winds.

Bridging the gap between construction completion and moving occupants into the workspace is known as **readiness planning**.

It's a multidisciplinary exercise in coordination, involving some of our internal colleagues and some of the professional team. Selecting the team will be our responsibility. We often call the team a **working group**, because we do things, rather than just talk about other people doing things.

It may appear obvious, but there are several aspects of readiness planning that create the best chance of success. We should:

- **Start early**: that is, earlier than we ever thought necessary. That usually means between 12 and 16 weeks before practical completion.
- **Be organised**: that is, know what needs to be done. Which is usually more than is initially anticipated. That includes keeping an accurate track of every single activity. Some individual items (particularly those requiring procurement of a technical system, for example an access control system) can be an entire project in themselves. Fortunately, there's a tool for this, described below.
- Understand the **dependencies**: while it's tricky to 'hyperlink' all the complex relationships between tasks, there will be some critical dependencies of which the team will need to be aware.

The following areas of activity are recommended to be included and can form the initial basis of a **readiness tracker**. The considerations are examples of what might be covered. Remember, at this stage the workspace has been designed and is in construction, and we've ordered most of our IT and furniture.

In practice, a readiness tracker will feature 10 to 15 items for most areas, usually resulting in over around 350–400 items in total. We've covered the vast majority in some context in this book. If it doesn't, it probably needs more thought. It's a daunting prospect, but by no means insurmountable if we're organised. The areas are, as a minimum:

- **Delivery**
  - Construction
  - Technology
  - Access
  - Sustainability
  - Furniture.
- **Change**
  - Occupancy
  - Engagement

- o Branding
- o Notifications
- o Landlord issues.
- **Service**
  - o Strategy
  - o Health and safety
  - o Maintenance
  - o Security
  - o Cleaning
  - o Catering
  - o Meeting rooms
  - o Front of house
  - o Logistics.
- **Occupation**
  - o Move-out
  - o Move-in
  - o Onboarding
  - o Day 1 plan
  - o Week 1 plan
  - o Events.
- **Post-move**
  - o Day 2 plan
  - o Close out
  - o Post-occupancy.

Each section will need an assigned owner. The tracker should allow for a RAG (red/amber/green) status to be applied to each issue – with each item initially set at grey ('not started') – and a space for an update comment. Siting in a shared online workspace allows the relevant section owner to update the tracker weekly. Ensuring the updates happen is down to us, with regular reminders to section owners; not just of the task, but of the value the working group is bringing.

THINGS TO LOOK OUT FOR

Here are some of the things to look out for in this area, to challenge or avoid wherever possible:

- **'Tendering = saving'**: at the time of writing, the days of the magical power of putting a requirement in the market and watching costs ratchet down in a competitive frenzy are over. In the current economic climate, global supply chains have become far less predictable; in some areas, costs can actually increase during a tender, as clarifications are sought and obtained.
- **'We just want to …'**: changes to construction, furniture, key building systems and technology once procured and in motion can seem small and easy to action but are never 'just' something. Delivery is a complex, interrelated system, and any additional request can impact the plan. Doing something else means not doing what was planned. Which means delay and cost. We must minimise changes once we're under way.
- **'We can't think of everything'**: but we can. Rather, we must. There's enough workspace creation experience in the world to ensure it's possible. The problem is that a list is too often created as a response to events beginning to run out of control. There's also often too much reliance placed on workstream success, without being conscious of how vital coordination between them is.

8

ACTIVATE
HOW WILL WE MAKE THE MOST
OF OUR WORKSPACE?

During this stage of project, we're going to explain to our colleagues how the workspace has been designed, and the opportunities it offers to work in new and different ways.

HOW DO WE MANAGE THE CHANGE?

As we noted in Part I, our change process began with the first inkling that there may be a project, irrespective of when we first formally announced it was happening. We'll have been continuing this process since, both formally and informally.

As with design and project management, our change managers will have a tailorable plan and series of tools that can be deployed. While this short book can't cover all aspects of leading the change to a new workspace, it can offer some principles and components of change, a range of activities that we should expect to see happen, and some thoughts on creating positive colleague behaviour.

DOI: 10.4324/9781003442684-11

Principles of change

There are five key principles of leading change in the workplace, that we might use to guide our approach and activity:

1 **Primacy**: as mentioned in Part I, where the vision for the new workspace was considered, as project leaders we're first and foremost leaders of change, and workspace practitioners second. Change is our primary discipline. We must never lose sight of this fact.

2 **Adaptation**: we're not trying to change people. Our aim is to give our colleagues the tools, knowledge and resources to adapt to a new working environment and/or ways of working. This is adaptation. It's not to be confused with adoption, which means sticking things on – with the risk they may fall off. Some won't adapt, however, but the goal is never to try to achieve 100% adaptation. There'll always be colleagues who don't want to change, or don't like what's proposed. We'll never convince everyone, and we shouldn't try to as it consumes too much time and energy on the team's part. Dissenting voices can be useful to us, too, as they offer insight, so we should never try to close them down.

3 **Patience**: change is experiential, and therefore takes time. While in creating a new workspace and moving our colleagues to it a clear cut-over date is set, for many of our colleagues no matter what we tell them and how we engage before the move, the reality will only become apparent when they're in the new workspace. The importance of example, therefore, can't be overstated. People will instinctively watch what others do, far more than listen to what they say. Especially their managers and leaders. Therefore, any new behaviours we wish to encourage in our new workspace must be role-modelled by senior leaders. Setting the right standards is hugely powerful.

4 **Preparation** first, a plan second. And our plan needs to remain flexible as we learn more over time. There's a simple hierarchy we can observe, based on the amount of information we have:

   a. For what we know we know: a **plan**.

  b. For what we know we don't know: a plan with **options**, based on likely outcomes.

  c. For what we don't know we don't know: **preparation**. We have no idea what's likely to happen, but we need to be ready for as many eventualities as possible.

  d. For what we don't know we know: or rather, what we're in denial of – **facing up** to the challenges we know exist. This may often be the most difficult of the four.

5 **Appraisal**: we're seeking an open dialogue with, and critical participation from, our colleagues, not 'buy-in'. Our change project isn't a transactional balance sheet, where we try and move everyone into the 'won over' column and hope they stay there. We're the easiest people to convince it's a great idea, and sometimes we need what's not working or advisable to be pointed out to us by our colleagues.

We can use these principles as a test for everything we decide to do.

TRUE STORY

The organisation's new workspace was well designed, responsive and rich in features and amenities. But very little had been conveyed to the occupants before 'live' day – a couple of town halls only. The effort had instead gone into creating a comprehensive 'welcome pack'. However, by the time the occupants walked through the door on day one, the information provided was ignored. There was simply too much to take in at one time. The team of helpers were besieged with questions, and frustration mounted. Leaving it all to the last minute – however impressive the product – didn't give colleagues time to think, process and adapt.

Components of change

We mentioned in Part II – where we looked at our initial message informing colleagues of the project – that change comprises three things, all of which will be happening simultaneously, and are related:

1 **Awareness**: our colleagues **know** what's happening, when, and what it means for them.
2 **Engagement**: our colleagues **feel** positive about the change.
3 **Involvement**: our colleagues **do** something beneficial for themselves and to help others, sometimes when asked and sometimes voluntarily.

We can divide the things we'll do to help our colleagues understand the new workspace into each of the three components.

Change activity

The basic package of things we might do include the following, noting that this is not an exhaustive list:

- **Awareness**:
  - The project **vision** and **objectives**, as we covered in Part I, in 'message house' or similar format.
  - **Creative stock** – logo(s), images and templates, tone of voice and lexicon. This should include the design of a regular e-mail (or other communications channel) project bulletin.
  - A detailed set of **questions and answers** (Q&As), that will be kept 'live' and added to on a rolling basis throughout the project. Some colleagues will want or need the detail. It also helps the team ensure *we* know the answers to all questions likely to be asked – it's a useful checklist. There'll be somewhere in the region of 70–100 by the time we've engaged with colleagues and thought everything through.
  - A little later in our project, a complete and consistent **new workplace guide**, an A–Z of all features, amenities and services. Like a 5-star hotel services directory. Ideally it should be online, and enable search and display by just the subject of interest, as no-one is likely to want to read (or trawl through) a huge and fairly dry document of this nature.

- **Engagement**:
  - o An **exhibition** or showcase, preferably both 'in real life' with 10–12 display boards, and online, covering all key aspects of the new workspace: why, where, what and how it'll work, who is involved and when it'll happen.
  - o A **pilot space** showing what the new workspace will look like, housed in our existing space – even to a limited extent, with colours, carpets and flooring, lighting and key items of furniture – is incredibly powerful. It can also act as a 'base' for future engagement activities.
  - o A **guide for managers**, taking them through the design and intended functionality of the new workspace, addressing what the opportunities will be for working differently, and what's needed of them in the coming months. We can then provide a pack for them to brief their teams and check back with us afterwards. It's incredibly important for colleagues to hear the message from their own leaders rather than everything being conveyed from the 'centre'.
  - o A **guide for executive assistants** and key personal assistants, who often face very different challenges to the rest of our colleagues. Their insight is also extremely important.
  - o **Day-in-the-life** stories, depicting different colleagues' journey from arrival to departure, taking in their use of various worksettings and amenities, and their interactions with colleagues. These are especially useful where greater mobility among shared spaces is a desired outcome.
  - o **Stories from the present**: where a short story or video is created capturing the thoughts, plans, experiences and aspirations of colleagues as the project unfolds.
  - o **Stories from the future** where a short story or video is created depicting the positives of life in the new workspace as imagined in (say) a year's time.
- **Involvement**:
  - o Design **interns**: where a small number of colleagues join the core team to help define and refine design elements.

- As previously mentioned, **clear outs** are a vital way to get everyone involved in readying for the move. They can be gamified, and prizes awarded.
- **Naming** conventions: whereby our colleagues are involved in suggesting names for key amenities of the workspace, meeting rooms, zones and some worksettings.
- **Onboarding** tours: everyone will need to be onboarded into the new workspace before they can be permitted to work there, and so we'll need to organise and script our tours and ensure access passes (actual or virtual) aren't provided until this has happened. If it's possible, our change champions should undertake the tours. This is covered in more detail shortly.
- **Day 1** and **week 1** support and activity planning. Extra helpers will be needed to handle request and fault logs, and to run events and organise catering. And, of course, the obligatory 'Here to help!' tee shirts for the team. The authors each have a collection.

The important aspect of a change programme is that it always remains flexible. Even the process of undertaking each of these activities changes the landscape, and so what may have once seemed like a good idea may need modifying or re-thinking. Which means we need to keep listening and always remember to 'read the room'.

TRUE STORY

Several activities needed to be completed by colleagues before the big move to the new workspace, that was about to accommodate several thousand people. At the same time, the team were receiving many requests for a tour of the building before the works were complete. A member of the team suggested a card with stickers be produced – if colleagues collected a sticker from each of the five activities, they were asked to complete to attend a site tour, it would help completion and limit tour numbers. The team were sceptical, as it seemed unlikely many people would take part. Over a thousand completed cards were presented! They all got a tour.

HOW DO WE ENCOURAGE THE RIGHT COLLEAGUE BEHAVIOUR?

Views differ on the approach that might be taken to how we achieve desired colleague behaviour in the new workspace, from complete 'laissez faire' (doing nothing and hoping it works out) to a fully guided and instructed programme, complete with a list of dos and don'ts. Sometimes the specifics of how colleagues are expected to behave are referred to as **protocols** and the overall approach as workspace **etiquette**.

It's important not to forget that at some stage, the current workspace once had an *intended* etiquette. Yet over time, whether conscious or not, people find ways that work for them within a workspace, and an *actual* behaviour set settles in for everyone. Paths, or shortcuts, of this nature are called **desire lines**, a term borrowed from the trails that animals tread in the wild as new paths are created, usually the shortest (and safest) route between two points. Humans tread them too – we often see them in parks and on college campuses.

These behaviours are also often accompanied by unwritten 'ground rules', ways of behaving that may not make sense to an external observer or the original designer of the workspace.

The fear is always that despite our investment in a new workspace, the least appealing habits and patterns will either carry over or return later when a 'steady state' has been reached and the project team stood down. Albeit deciding what is 'good' and 'bad' behaviour requires exploration and consensus.

During the strategy and design phases we'll no doubt have modelled – either actually or in our minds – the **ideal occupant** of our new workspace. Our ideal occupant will likely:

- Only use worksetting for as long as they need and clear their stuff away when they go – and not leave items behind to reserve it for later use (often termed 'beach towelling').
- Moderate the volume of their voice in open workspace.
- Take phone and online calls away from their desk, in a worksetting suited for the purpose.
- Not eat food at a desk – or smelly food anywhere in the workspace!
- Use worksettings for the appropriate number of people (such as meeting rooms and informal spaces).

Of course, the ideal occupant doesn't exist, and our colleagues will rarely be as perfect as we modelled – thank goodness!

Yet rather than a set of instructions or other form of highly prescriptive approach, we can encourage our colleagues to be **good neighbours**. The appeal of this approach is that we tap into instinctive attitudes and behaviours. When asking different groups of people for examples of what neighbourly behaviour in a workspace means, the authors always get similar results.

This also supports the idea of 'neighbourhoods' as discreet physical areas of our workspace, covered in Part II.

Neighbourliness, as it may be called, has six key characteristics:

1 **Considerate**: putting the needs of others before our own when required, and judging when the time is right to do so.
2 **Respectful**: balancing our regard of our colleagues, our workspace and the environment, taking none for granted.
3 **Proactive**: taking the initiative, not always waiting for others to act or assuming they will.
4 **Aware**: knowing what's going on around us when our colleagues may need help or where we may need to act on a risk or problem.
5 **Visible**: being available for when our colleagues need our help, advice or input (even though there will be times when we need to focus).
6 **Flexible**: understanding that in different contexts and at different times our behaviour needs to be modified. This characteristic has come to the fore since the pandemic, given far more variable patterns of use of workspace. For example, a 'no calls at the desk' guide would work on a busy Tuesday but would make little sense on a Friday afternoon.

What we're hoping to convey to colleagues therefore is the need to be aware of what's going on and exercise neighbourly judgment. Essentially, to be decent and caring human beings. What's not to like about such an aim?

HOW DO WE HANDLE RESISTANCE?

We and our stakeholders may be excited about our new workspace, but not everyone might. We're about to break established patterns and desire lines, some of which may have been formed over many years. The authors are often asked how we deal with resistance to our new workspace, whether intentional or not.

Typical areas our colleagues could be concerned about are:

- A change of physical **location**, where a move is involved. It may be less convenient for them or increase journey time and cost.
- A change from assigned seating to **shared** workspace, creating a feeling of loss of something familiar or supportive of a routine.
- A loss of **amenity**, such as the replacement of a full-service restaurant with a grab-and-go cafe or self-service offer.
- The introduction of a new **technology** that may be seen as a loss of freedom through tracking usage or attendance.

TRUE STORY

The headquarters of a large organisation was relocating to a new workspace, and a lot of senior and middle managers were giving up their private offices. Most of them, unwillingly. Some hysterically. Such was the fear of noise and disturbance in the new, more open environment that a physically separated 24-seat library and concentration area was created, complete with an external terrace. Talking and phones were banned. Yet a full year after occupying the new workspace the area was converted to a project room – not a single person had used it at any time. Most fears rarely materialise, but we often have to prove them to be unfounded.

Here are some suggestions for managing perceived resistance:

- **Listen** and **understand**: what is often perceived as stubbornness may simply be the result of the pace of the transition. The views expressed often contain valuable insight. There's always a reason for the objection, and we need to understand it. Sometimes our colleagues just need to know they've been heard.
- **Frame**: we mustn't see adjusting to change as 'resistance' (unless, of course it involves planned obstruction) but rather as our colleagues absorbing what we're proposing and processing what it

may mean for them. Framing it in this way also helps to avoid using the language of resistance. It also helps colleagues to contextualise their issues – seeing themselves in a different environment can help them re-frame their concerns as opportunities.

- **Layer**: communicate, engage and involve early and often. Change is iterative, and perceived resistance at a point of the project may be about something specific and may not mean an objection to the whole transition.
- **Affirm**: focus on the opportunities the new workspace offers (the gains), rather than what will no longer be available or possible (the loss). This will positively shape the dialogue. It means taking care of what we say and how we say it, as expressing in the negative is easy to do.

It's important to remember that change management isn't a form of magic, but an entirely human discipline. It's possible we may do all of the above and a colleague will still oppose the move to the new workspace. At that point, it'll be for them to decide what to do.

WHAT HAPPENS AT THE COMPLETION OF CONSTRUCTION?

The last week of construction and the first weeks in which the workspace is in our possession can be frenetic. We'll have a general contractor trying to finish and leave, while we'll be itching to get in and set up. Teams from the various movers and installers will need to work in the same areas. There'll be tension and emotion. It's a period that will warrant our focus and involvement.

The four weeks around this period often look something like Figure 8.1.

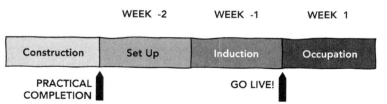

Figure 8.1 Typical end-of-project schedule.

In the last week of construction there will be:

- Final finishing and dressing of the workspace.
- Final testing and commissioning of services (water, heating, lighting, air conditioning etc.).
- Training of our FM team in how to manage the services.
- Snagging of construction.
- Furniture installation, new – by the dealer.
- Audiovisual installation completion.
- 'Sparkle' (thorough) clean.

As mentioned in Part I, this all ends at practical completion (PC). Note that PC will only be granted if in the view of the contract administrator it is, other than for minor matters, finished. At PC, the workspace is handed over to our organisation.

In the first week of occupation there will be:

- Potential snagging over-run (by arrangement – potentially out of hours).
- Furniture installation, re-used items – by the move contractor.
- IT desktop install, new kit.
- IT desktop install, re-used kit.
- Stocking up – resource areas, stationery, kitchens, etc.
- Planting installation.
- Signage, wayfinding and branding installation.

All of which means a micro-plan for the week either side of PC will be essential.

Depending on what needs to be done, it's possible that some tasks that would have been intended to happen before (or after) PC happen after (or before). The logical sequence must make sense. Anything happening before PC will be done under the management of the general contractor, with PPE requirements in place.

There will also need to be protection applied to all finished surfaces by any contractor installing anything – lumps being knocked out of freshly painted walls and damage to flooring aren't uncommon during moves and furniture installation. In which case having one of the general contractor's decorators on hand can be useful.

At the end of the first week of the workspace in our possession, it'll be fully ready for occupation. We're ready to bring our colleagues in to see it and be inducted.

Of course, this assumes that all our workspace is ready at the same time. There are two situations where this may not be the case:

- What is termed **sectional completion** of a workspace where only some is available to us, and we obtain **partial possession**. This may have been intended from the outset or may be agreed closer to completion as an expedient measure where delays or unforeseen issues have meant the space cannot all be made available at once.
- Where we are renovating our space in situ, in a phased plan.

In both instances, careful planning will be necessary. There may be an extra engagement challenge with our colleagues, who may be exposed to construction work (and the associated noise and other impacts) in close proximity for a period of time.

IS ONBOARDING NECESSARY?

Just like the safety briefing when we get on an aeroplane, the **onboarding** or **induction** is not a step to skip under time pressure. In some countries, it's a legal requirement, while in most countries it's accepted best practice.

- **Why**: there are several reasons:
  - It provides people with essential health and safety information. In the case of fire evacuation, it could be lifesaving.
  - For most people, it'll be the first time they'll have been in the new workspace, and so it's valuable orientation that will save time and remove any confusion on day one.
  - For the project team, it's an opportunity to remind colleagues of the function and features of the workspace, and to explain how their needs and aspirations have been translated into this physical reality.

- **How**: a physical tour of the building at a designated and booked time conducted to a pre-prepared script by a suitably knowledgeable member of the project team, usually lasting around an hour.
- **What**: the tour will:
  - o Identify all key health and safety features and processes, especially those related to security and fire evacuation.
  - o Identify all key features, amenities, services and technology in the new space.
  - o Recap on all information provided to date – including worksettings, meeting spaces, lockers and storage, neighbourly behaviour, and anything specifically different from the existing workspace.
  - o Confirm the right of the attendee to work in the new space through the issue of an access card or mobile phone access credentials.

If we feel we need a booking request system (useful for all but the smallest workspaces) it should have the ability to manage changes to appointments and a log of all those attending.

A process for continuing onboarding after opening will therefore be needed as there'll be those unable to attend during the allotted time. Onboarding isn't just for those colleagues initially relocating – every new joiner thereafter will need to be inducted. A regular weekly slot is the usual way of handling the on-going need.

THINGS TO LOOK OUT FOR

Here are some of the things to look out for in this area, to challenge or avoid wherever possible:

- **'Build the workspace, do the change'**: the authors have often been invited to lead workspace change too late in the programme. Just as with communications, change isn't something we 'do', and certainly isn't something we do when everything else that's important has been decided. Workspace change leaders are often subject matter experts, too, with valuable perspectives and experience of what works and what doesn't. Why would we want to bring only them in when they can't make a difference?

- **'Tell them what to do!'**: if we're not careful, our emotional attachment to the project, in particular our desire to see the workspace working as we've imagined, can create an undue focus on our part on people doing what we ask of them. We may not see this shift in our own behaviour, as it, too, will adapt over time. Yet we don't want to be walking through our new workspace with a cattle prod, telling our colleagues to move about and not 'hog' a worksetting. Where something's happening with which we may not agree, the appeal will always be to the neighbourly spirit of our colleagues. We need to allow them to decide for themselves that it's the right thing to do.
- **'Reinvent everything!'**: There's often a sense with a new workspace that everything must change, that nothing can carry over from our existing environment. The desire for change for its own sake can gather momentum. Yet much of what happens today works, the desire lines have been formed and our colleagues have found ways to make it easy for themselves. We've observed them in action. So, we must be bold enough to change what needs changing, and assured enough to retain what works. As it's a matter of judgment, we won't always get it right – but simply reinventing everything is dangerous way of avoiding making decisions.

9

EVOLVE
HOW WILL WE LIVE WITH
OUR NEW WORKSPACE?

We've created our new workspace, and now we're working in it and loving it. But it's never finished. In our final stage, we'll need to consider how we plan for effective operation, and what we need to do to ensure the workspace adapts with the needs of our organisation and colleagues, to ensure it's always relevant.

HOW WILL WE OPERATE OUR WORKSPACE?

The journey for our colleagues begins at the point we open the doors to our new workspace. Designing and planning for the continual efficient and effective operation of our workspace over time is therefore vital.

We may already have a facilities management (FM) team, in which case they'll have been involved in the project from the outset. But we'll need to be aware of the wide range of issues that require consideration to ensure our workspace works, all the time. This is especially so with expectations of an increased provision of amenities and services in workspace. FM is no longer the 'back of house' function it once was.

DOI: 10.4324/9781003442684-12

What is facilities management?

FM is as old as buildings. It emerged as a discipline in the 1990s from a mishmash of similar functions with differing names, such as administration and housing services. FM is effectively an umbrella, covering a vast array of professions with their own educational and vocational paths, organisations and professional bodies. It's a function most evident when it's not there or fails, rather than when it's successful. Because we can't see things happening it doesn't mean they're not.

The services included within FM are commonly divided in organisational terms into 'hard' (building-related, noisy, greasy and hidden) and 'soft' (human, visible and accessible) services, but this belies the fact that most services are a combination of both elements. A split between what we might term **management** (enabling) and **operations** (doing) is more helpful.

Since its emergence as a discipline in its own right, FM has continued to evolve. Many years ago, it would have expected to include telecommunications, car fleets and smoking rooms. Post-pandemic, the role of FM has in some organisations has been combined with other disciplines such as HR and operations to form a broader support function termed **workplace experience** or similar, taking it from 'managing facilities' to facilitating safe, healthy, creative and engaging workspaces. Today, we find prominence is given to, among other services, wellbeing, 'green' travel and sustainability.

Even where the FM function hasn't combined with others within the organisation, a number of the services provided involve degrees of interface or collaboration with other functions within the organisation. Health, safety, environment and wellbeing (HSEW) for instance has an overlap with human resources and legal. In non-office locations, such as production facilities, FM may be fully integrated with the core business of the organisation, as it may extend to critical systems and machinery.

The list does not include those areas of responsibility common to all leadership roles including vision and goal setting, staff management, recruitment, transfer of staff to/from outsource partners, training and certification, change management and performance management.

Figure 9.1 has been kept succinct but still comprises 80 areas of responsibility, all of which may apply to a small building or portfolio as much as those that are extensive in scale. It's by no means exclusive, and by the same token, several of the services may not apply to our workspace.

Management

ADMINISTRATION	ENGAGEMENT	HSEW	REAL ESTATE	PROJECTS
Budgets	Service strategy	Contractors	Statutory & legal	CAD library
Reporting	Services guide	Compliance	Lease obligations	Space planning
Procurement	Communication	Registers	Landlord liaison	Small works
Contracts	Requirements	Managing risk	Rent reviews	Relocation
Uniforms/PPE	Forecasting	Accidents	Local tax reviews	Furniture
Insurance	Utilisation	First Aid	Parking	Equipment
Asset registers	Special needs	Sustainability	Local authorities	O&M
Benchmarking	Research	Wellbeing	Green travel	Warranties

Operations

TECHNICAL SERVICES			COLLEAGUE SERVICES	
MAINTENANCE	SECURITY	CLEANING	FRONT OF HOUSE	LOGISTICS
BMS	Access policy	Office cleaning	Reception	Mailroom
Building fabric	Access control	Window cleaning	Visitor process	Couriers
Plant & systems	Manned guarding	Specialist cleans	Meeting rooms	Goods inwards
PPM system	CCTV	Deep cleans	Catering	Porterage
Fire safety	Keys	Washrooms	Hospitality	Reprographics
Handyman	Evacuation plans	Waste	Retail	Storage
Landscaping	Bug sweeps	Recycling	Service desk	Offsite archiving
Utilities & energy	Chauffeurs	Pest control	Event support	Vehicles

Figure 9.1 Facilities Management areas of responsibility.

Some of the abbreviations used are:

- BMS: building management system
- CAD: computer aided design
- CCTV: closed circuit television
- O&M: operations and maintenance
- PPE: personal protective equipment
- PPM: planned preventive maintenance.

TRUE STORY

A well-meaning FM of a large drinks brand referred to colleagues as her 'children'. She prided herself and her team on being the guardians of the workspace. Although talented and committed to their work, being mothered by the FM team brought out the rebellious side of colleagues, resulting in a boycott of the Christmas party and an incident involving a pigeon and the downstairs kitchen (the pigeon wasn't harmed). Rather than culturing an adult–adult relationship, the parent-child approach brought about unintended behaviours and problems. As W. C. Fields once said – never work with animals or children.

What approaches to FM are possible?

It'll be vital to have our FM suppliers on board early. The more they can support the design of our workspace for operation, the better the outcome is likely to be.

An extensive FM supply industry can meet almost all service requirements through a variety of delivery models. There's no perfect delivery model – only what's right for the organisation. Essentially the scale of the workspace portfolio often dictates the approach taken, beginning with the smallest of organisations managing their workspace 'in house'.

- **In house**: all services are performed by direct employees of the organisation. While it ensures control and potentially staff commitment and loyalty, it's management intensive, and the comparative insularity can prevent exposure to new ideas or practices.

- **Key task contracts**: the organisation tenders and manages key service contracts (usually maintenance, security and cleaning – sometimes catering, if provided). While this offers flexibility and the potential to select 'best-in-class' (if such a thing can be said to exist) operators, it takes a lot of management time and can yield little cost leverage.
- **Single task contract**: the organisation tenders and manages a single contract for all key services. The single point of responsibility and economies of scale can be beneficial, but it also creates a single point of failure, too (along with the options below).
- **Total FM, self-delivery**: All services are provided by one supplier, delivered by direct employees of the supplier. The economies of scale and flexibility must be balanced against the potential for the quality of some services to be stronger than others.
- **Total FM, managing agent**: All services are provided by one supplier, who sub-contract and manage specialist service providers as required. This approach can ensure best in class task providers and economies of scale, but there may be additional management costs.

Landlord services

In a shared building, the landlord will also have an FM team on board for the management of the building, its common parts and any tenant services provided. Contacting the landlord team early will be essential.

Where our workspace is small, we may be able to extend the landlord service team's task-level contracts (such as cleaning) to our own workspace, which can have logistical and cost advantages.

Most landlord service teams produce a **guide for tenants** that details what they do and any requirements of tenant organisations occupying workspace in the building. It covers areas such as access and security, reception, fire safety, cleaning, parking, cycling and showers. It also details requirements that will need to be adhered to when we undertake any works in our workspace. If the guide isn't offered early, it may need to be requested.

The guide may contain items that impact our workspace design. For instance, the sorting requirements for recycled material may need to be understood before bins and counter-top holes are specified in our cafe or kitchen space. It'll also contain content that will need to be included in our **workplace guide** referenced earlier in Part III.

HOW DO WE KNOW IF OUR WORKSPACE IS WORKING?

Having invested considerable time, energy and money in creating a new workspace, it'll be important to note at a future juncture whether it's been successful. While there may be executive impatience with proving its worth, it's always better to allow at least 3 – preferably 6 – months for people to settle. We may choose to impose a **change freeze** during this period, for all bar emergencies, to avoid having to respond to 'knee-jerk' reactions.

Following this period, we might then choose to undertake a formal **post-occupancy evaluation** (POE) of our workspace. It's an odd expression and should perhaps just be called 'occupancy evaluation'.

It's a beneficial exercise for the following reasons:

- Did the **reality** meet **expectations**? Our colleagues told us what they needed and hoped for. While we engaged with them throughout, shaping the workspace to suit their needs and wishes wherever possible, it's worth validating that what they asked for we did, and did well. It's a respectful gesture to those who offered valuable insight.
- We can formally measure our success against our **KPIs** described in Part II. This is a vital closing step in our audit trail for the investment.
- If our organisation carries any formal financial, governance, quality or confidentiality accreditation or **certification**, it may be a requirement of such.
- It forms part of our **learning** as a team, as we may be moving onto another workspace project after this.

- It can point to what we may need **more of** (what's working) and what we may need to **adjust** or remove (what isn't) as part of the evolution of the workspace.
- It formally confirms that the project is complete and that we're in 'business as usual'. As far as anything is 'usual'!

There are several issues to be aware of with POE, too:

- We're going to be dealing with **low levels of interest** at this time – unless there are significant problems – compared to the expectations and excitement around the possibility of creating new workspace. It'll feel like a project that's complete, that doesn't need re-visiting. Incentives to take part may therefore be necessary.
- It's a **point-in-time** exercise, with all the issues inherent with such. Timing will be everything. Where we can make the exercise more an 'occupancy evaluation' – in real time – the better. **Pulse surveys**, brief (1–2 minute) questionnaires on specific matters over a longer period, can go some way to resolving this.
- Gauging success is difficult. What **margins** constitute success? Everything that's positive? If, for example, overall satisfaction with the workspace increased by 11%, is that a 'win'?
- What happens if the POE shows that our new workspace **isn't working** in many respects? What do we do? On the plus side, at least we'll know, and have pointers as to where to start.

POE usually comprises a mix of subjective and objective measures, similar in many respects to the work undertaken in the early predesign stages of our project. We can either undertake some or all of it ourselves or pay a workspace consultant or designer to complete it:

- **Subjective**:
  - **Satisfaction**: via a survey. We may repeat the questions asked of our previous workspace and compare scores (hopefully to see an improvement).
  - **Effectiveness**: interviews with key **stakeholders**.
  - **Ease of use**: focus **groups** with a mix of colleagues.

- **Objective**:
  - **Attendance patterns**: via a utilisation study, as covered in Part I and mentioned below.
  - **Usage patterns**: via a manual study or sensors, observing which worksettings are used for what activity and frequency.
  - **Ethnography**: observing patterns and modes of behaviour and studying worksetting use.
  - **Organisational benefit**: understanding the contribution the workspace is making to the organisation – essentially, its reason for existing. Which means, what value it's delivering over and above everyone working remotely, using a set of agreed measures?

The last of these measures – organisational benefit – has typically been a challenge for those in the business of creating workspace because it's inherently tied to the nature and function of the organisation, on which data or information is not always available.

To this extent, therefore, we must work with colleagues within the organisation from the outset to establish how we might create and report on such measures. They may include, dependent upon the nature of the functions occupying the workspace:

- Output (productivity) – specific or collective measures
- Sales
- Client/customer interaction
- Cross-selling opportunities
- Relationship creation and development
- Inter-team initiatives
- Innovations (new products or services) that reach market
- People attraction and retention
- Net promoter score (NPS) if used
- Ratings in online employee applications.

When complete, our POE is typically reported back to our SteerCo, with an action plan generated to address areas of concern or where helpful suggestions have been made.

HOW DO WE 'FUTURE PROOF' OUR WORKSPACE?

We can't future proof anything about our workspace – we're dealing with 'unknown unknowns', as we referenced previously. But we can future-prepare.

We referenced in Part I a key challenge in developing a strategy for our workspace is balancing the needs of today with aspirations for the future. The past and present are often much easier to capture, understand and represent than the vagaries and unpredictability of the future. The conundrum is:

- In reflecting the **present**, it renders the outcome recognisable and makes it easier for our colleagues to 'associate' with what's being provided. But in doing so it may entrench existing attitudes and methods, in the medium to long-term acting as a brake on the organisation as it evolves.
- In depicting the **future**, the process of 'acting as if' may not be as associable immediately but it creates a tangible signal of intent. However, the organisation may not evolve as expected, meaning our workspace becomes increasingly less relevant over time.

We've mentioned previously that our workspace is a journey not a product – it's forever in 'beta trial' mode, a living experiment. Or **perpetual beta** as it's called in the world of software development. Which is why we set out to create a workspace flexible enough in terms of scale, worksettings and reconfigurability to be able to meet the needs of today and tomorrow.

When our colleagues occupy their new workspace, two key things will happen, both of which aren't to be unduly concerned about as they're a natural outcome of providing varied workspace and giving permission to colleagues to explore it:

1   Not **all our worksettings** will be successful. The workspace is highly unlikely to fail in full, but some worksettings will turn out to be more usable and popular than others. Which means we'll either need to proactively demonstrate the value of those not being used as much as other spaces, (it may be that the value hasn't been recognised yet or we may not have

been clear enough on their purpose), or tweak the balance of worksettings.

2 The success of **some worksettings** will impact the use of others. Providing a central cafe, for example, with 'high street' quality coffee is likely to impact the use of localised kitchenettes with an inferior or 'fast lane' offer. Similarly, diner booths with high backs may mean little use of 'huddle' tables in open workspace.

Future-preparing a workspace can involve the following considerations, both regarding its design and specification, and on-going operation:

- In terms of designing and specifying the workspace for flexibility:
  o Ensuring that we don't 'hard construct' too many installations, enabling changes to be made easily as required. This means providing as many **free-standing** installations as possible, even if they require time to relocate. It doesn't mean everything needs to be on wheels, just that it doesn't need to be demolished if not required in its present form or location.
  o Ensuring that as many installations as possible are **proprietary** and are likely to have continuity of production and maintenance for several years ahead. This can be checked at the time of their procurement. It's an argument for minimising the amount of joinery installed and using 'off the shelf' furniture instead, albeit this can have a negative impact on the look, feel and uniqueness of our workspace.
  o Ensuring the **building systems** can be easily and cheaply adapted – heating, cooling, fresh air, lighting and fire safety installations such as smoke detection and sprinklers. They're often the most problematic and hence expensive barriers to workspace flexibility.
- In terms of assessing the performance of the workspace in operation, following on from our POE exercise:
  o Maintaining a regular and open **dialogue** with occupants of the space to ensure its needs and suitability are

constantly re-evaluated. They'll be 'co-designers' as we go forward. Sometimes our effective communication channels are closed when a project is complete, in the belief they're no longer necessary – it may not be these specific channels we keep open, but alternatives will be needed.

o   Building questions related to the workspace into any ongoing organisational **engagement surveys** or data capture, usually run by HR.

o   Creating the means to capture ongoing **attendance** at the workspace and **utilisation** of space and worksettings, either manually or using technology (manual, access control installations, sensors or camera-based systems, or via our IT network).

o   Maintaining our study of the **organisational benefits** of our workspace, captured in our KPIs, as a real time insight tool. As our organisation evolves, so will the performance and relevance of our workspace: it must continue to work for the organisation and its people.

All of which means a requirement for the workspace project to continue. Learning about how to best use a workspace is often cumulative, creating a 'ratchet effect' where each successful change lays the foundation for another. The continuance of the project may be a task picked up by the FM team, in which case we may need to work with them on the go-forward plan, or by another function within the organisation. Either way, in short, it's never over!

HOW CAN WE SUPPORT REMOTE COLLEAGUES?

This book has been all about creating physical workspace, with the high probability that it'll be an environment designed and operated to enable and support hybrid working. While there's a wealth of resource available on how to lead, manage, support and engage remote colleagues, it's worth including some considerations here. Organisations need to be aware that their legal and ethical responsibilities to remote workers are just the same as for those based primarily in the workspace.

The following factors can be considered as a minimum, demanding of a cross-functional programme to deliver and maintain:

- **Culture**:
  - Policy and procedure: formal/informal arrangements, prescriptive/discretionary guidance and clarity on levels of flexibility.
  - Management: information, regular planned and responsive contact, workload assessment, performance management and pastoral care.
  - Inclusion and equity: fair access to resources and opportunities. Equating the experience of colleagues not on-site with those that are.
  - Process: etiquette and expectations around working synchronously (at the same time) and asynchronously (at different times), to avoid pressure to work during ant-social hours.
  - Communication: two-way always-open channels and dialogue.
  - Learning and development: planning, access to information and training.
  - Financial support: allowances for heating, lighting, utilities and technology.
  - Alternative to home working: coworking membership.
- **Environment**:
  - Location: satisfaction with suitability of workspace, privacy, noise and disturbance, access to daylight and access to rest space. Re-assessment where circumstances change.
  - Remote set-up: ergonomic furniture, desk, chair and storage.
  - IT: connectivity, kit and access PC, monitor(s), peripherals, printing and secure access to apps/files.
  - Security: physical, personal and data.
- **Operation**:
  - IT help: repairs and replacement, software support.
  - Facilities help: stationery, postage, furniture repairs and replacement.

- o   Health and safety: ergonomic assessments, electrical safety.
- o   Data and security: printed material, data privacy.
- o   Departure ('offboarding') arrangements: clear guidance on what to do when leaving the organisation.

HOW DO WE MAINTAIN INTEREST IN THE WORKSPACE?

There was a time pre-pandemic when creating fantastic workspace was (almost, at least) all we needed to do, as our colleagues would be expected or required to be present for much of their working time.

In the era of hybrid working, where a choice of location exists, it's a combination of what we create and what happens within it that constitutes the draw. As mentioned earlier, our reason for being present may be to perform certain tasks using specialist equipment, or work with certain colleagues. Often, this only really requires a few days a week to be functionally present in our workspace.

Which means the organisation must do more to attract people and offer higher-value experiences on-site. Community may on occasion be created accidentally, but it often needs invigoration. When specifying and designing our workspace, we'll have considered the possibility of some or all the following happening on a regular basis:

- **Learning** and **development**: talks and seminars on organisational matters, general interest or motivation.
- **Low-key social events**: lunches, designated morning or afternoon breaks with tea/coffee and cake ('*fika*' as it's known in Sweden).
- **Organised social events**: gatherings, parties, celebrations and specific activities.
- **Town halls**: information broadcast on organisational performance and initiatives, with the opportunity to ask questions.
- **Interest pursuits**, with specialists: barista or cooking training (if the facilities exist), fashion design or gardening, for example.

- **Networking** and **relationship building**: specific activities designed to boost colleague contact.
- **Leadership access**: depending on the size and nature of the organisation, and possibly in association with one of the above initiatives, direct colleague access to leaders for questions and answers.

Of course, there are always straightforward incentives like free food. But with an active, community-minded organisation living and working in a fantastic workspace, we can probably do better than that. In fact, we really need to.

THINGS TO LOOK OUT FOR

Here are some of the things to look out for in this area, to challenge or avoid wherever possible:

- **'FM: it's just unblocking toilets'**: well, someone has to, especially when paper towels have been shoved down them despite the clearly displayed polite request not to. FM is an incredibly important operational discipline that is vital not just to keeping the lights on (and the toilets flushing) but to the day-to-day running of our new workspace. If our organisation has an FM team, involving them early and throughout will be vital. We owe them that.
- **'We need to mandate attendance'**: it's an easy response following significant investment in a new workspace and seeing variable attendance when occupied. We (and our SteerCo) could be forgiven for thinking it's so amazing everyone will be queuing around the block to get in every day. They won't be. The same preferences for hybrid working will likely remain, but we'll need to give our new workspace time to demonstrate its value. And we'll need to be a creative, active community-building organisation, too.
- **'We can go back to our day jobs when this is all over'**: well, yes and no. Now that we've led our workspace creation project, we'll be forever associated with it. It'll be our baby. We'll have an eye on how its working and how our colleagues

are using it every day. We'll notice when things aren't as they should be or working. We'll have a group of comrades who went on the journey with us, who will also be invested. And we'll probably have to resist the urge to get involved (until the next project comes around!). But that's because it's an emotional experience into which we'll have put heart and soul. But one, hopefully, we'll always look back on with pride. There's nothing quite like it.

Glossary of terms

Most of the terms listed have been covered at some stage during the book – a few have been added that you may hear at varying times throughout the project.

Acoustics
The study of how to maximise the benefits of sound and mitigate the negative effects of noise in the workspace.

Activity based workplace (ABW)
An approach to the workplace that provides for a wide range of shared worksettings to support specific defined activities, allowing occupants to move freely between them as required.

Agile workplace
An approach to the workplace that provides for a wide range of shared worksettings allowing occupants to move freely between them as required. Note that 'Agile' has a different meaning in the field of software development, denoting a specific work methodology.

Anthropology
The study of people, in particular their behaviour, cultures and societies in the past and present.

Artificial intelligence (AI)
The ability of a computer system to perform tasks normally requiring human intelligence and discernment.

Asynchronous work
The process of two or more people undertaking work on the same task or project at different times.

Back office
The space in which administrative and management functions are conducted, with little or no interaction with external parties.

Building management system (BMS)
Building control systems compromising monitoring hardware and software applications.

Building specification
The formal description of the scale, composition and operating systems of a building.

Bürolandschaft (office landscape)
An approach to workspace design developed in Germany in the late 1950s based on an organic representation of the flow of people and information in workspace.

Capital allowances
Tax reliefs available for capital expenditure in the creation of an asset of ongoing benefit for the organisation.

Category A
A standard of finish of a building enabling occupation, typically including raised floors, suspended ceilings, internal surfaces and basic mechanical and electrical services.

Category B
A standard of finish of a building beyond Category A enabling beneficial use, typically including lighting, flooring, interior partitions and doors, decorative finishes and joinery items.

Category C
A standard of finish of a building beyond Category B enabling day-to-day usage, including all loose items of furniture, fixtures and equipment.

Caves-and-commons (also: 'combi-office')
An approach to the workspace in which a choice is provided between cellular offices ('caves') and meeting rooms and shared, open space ('commons').

Collaboration
The process of actively working together, free of compulsion, to define and attain an outcome.

Cooperation
The process of actively working together to attain the same pre-defined and agreed outcome.

Coordination
The process of organising people or groups so that they work together effectively to attain the same pre-defined and agreed outcome.

Core and flex
An approach to real estate occupancy in which the majority of workspace is leased directly (core) by an organisation to meet known demand and an amount of additional space is rented on a short-term basis to allow for peaks and troughs in demand (flex).

Coworking
A shared workspace in which individuals or organisations purchase membership for a given period.

Defects liability period
A set period (usually a year) after a construction project has been completed during which a general contractor has the right to return to the site to remedy defects.

Design and build (D&B)
A procurement method in which a single general contractor is appointed to design and construct the entire workspace scheme.

Design brief
The detailed, documented nature of the client's requirements for a workspace.

Digital first
The creation, distribution and storage of information in digital format. May also mean the approach to work, encompassing philosophy, tools, methods and processes over physical space.

Dilapidations
The works required by a tenant to return workspace to a pre-agreed condition, or their agreed value, at the termination of a workspace lease.

Distributed working
A mode of working in which the physical place of work may be anywhere at any time, including but not restricted to those places of work designated by the organisation.

Ergonomics
The relationship between an individual and their surroundings and equipment.

Ethnography
The systematic study of individual cultures, usually by immersive observation.

Facilities management (FM)
The management of the built environment and other resources at both a strategic and day-to-day level to meet organisational objectives and maintain a safe and effective environment for people.

Fit-out
The process of making interior workspaces suitable for occupation and use.

Flexible working
The ability and permission to vary hours of work. Note that this varies by location, and different definitions often apply either in practice or in law.

Flexispace
A shared workspace comprising dedicated and common parts in which individuals or organisations purchase membership for a given period.

Furniture, fixtures and equipment (FF&E)
The moveable furniture, fixtures, and other equipment that have no permanent connection to the structure of a building.

Heads of terms (HoT)
A non-binding statement of key provisions in a proposed sale, partnership, lease or other agreement.

Hot-desking (also: free address)
Non-assigned worksettings in a workspace available for use as required.

Hotelling
Non-assigned worksettings in a workspace available for reserved use as required.

Hub-and-spoke
A real estate portfolio comprising a central urban location combined with several distributed suburban locations.

Hybrid working
A mode of working in which work may be undertaken at either the premises of the organisation or the home of the individual.

Internal area
The wall-to-wall area of a building able to be practicably used by its occupants, excluding building cores.

Key performance indicators (KPIs)
Quantifiable or qualifiable targets set against specific required actions.

Learning and development (L&D)
Activities undertaken by an organisation to further the knowledge, skills or experience of its employees.

Lease
An agreement by which one party conveys land, property or equipment to another for a specified time, usually in return for a periodic payment.

Licence to alter
A legal agreement between a tenant and a landlord of a building that grants the tenant approval to implement defined alterations to the leased area.

Location agnostic
An approach to operating an organisation or performing a role in which no commitment is made to regular physical premises.

Managing agent
The formal representative of the landlord of a building charged with ensuring it's managed and maintained to an agreed standard.

Minimum viable workplace (MVW)
A coherent and functional workplace derived from meeting only the fundamental specific needs of the organisation.

Office
The space within a building used for the purpose of commercial, professional or administrative work.

Open-plan
An approach to workspace in which the primary space in which work is undertaken is not physically subdivided.

People-centric
A focus on the needs, safety and comfort of people as a key outcome in the design and operation of workspace.

Personal protective equipment (PPE)
Wearable equipment intended to protect the body from harm.

Planned preventive maintenance (PPM)
The advanced scheduling and conduct of tasks intended to ensure equipment or buildings remain in full and safe working order

Portfolio (real estate)
Multiple property investments, either leased or owned.

Post-occupancy evaluation (POE)
The process of obtaining qualitative and quantitative data on how a workspace is performing in relation to its intended use.

Practical completion (PC)
The formal completion of a building or workspace to a condition enabling it to be legally and practically used as intended.

Private office
A worksetting fully enclosed on four sides accessed via a door.

Productivity
The effectiveness of effort as measured by the rate of output per unit of input.

Readiness planning
A co-ordinated approach to ensure that a building is fully functional for the purpose of occupation.

Refurbishment
The improvement of something, notably a building or workspace.

Remote working
See *distributed working*.

Rent-free period
A defined period during a lease during which the tenant is not required to pay rent, usually offered by the landlord as an incentive to commit to the lease.

Request for information (RFI)
A written request of a supplier of goods or services to obtain information about its standing, experience and capabilities.

Request for proposal (RFP)
A written request of a supplier of goods or services to detail their approach, methodology, resources and pricing to meet a specific defined need.

Satisfaction survey
A study designed to determine the level of user contentment with a product, service, process or situation.

Segmentation
The identification of particular common work patterns or functional types within a given group of people.

Serendipitous encounter
A chance meeting between one or more people in which the subject of the interaction is unplanned yet proves to be of potential further interest.

Serendipity
An unplanned or unintended fortunate discovery.

Serviced office
Fully fitted, equipped and managed workspace rented on a fixed fee basis.

Shell-and-core
The external building structure together with internal spaces for services (pipes, ducts and cable) and people circulation (stairs, elevators).

Site selection
The practice of determining the most appropriate geographical location for an organisation's operation.

Smart working
See Agile working.

Snagging
The identification and rectification of minor faults with construction or installation works.

Space allocation
The provision of definable areas of workspace for individuals and groups of people.

SteerCo (Steering Committee)
A group of senior and influential leaders within an organisation assembled for the purpose of making key decisions on a project including outcome and budget.

Surveyor
A professional person who examines the condition of land and buildings.

Useable space
The internal area of a building plus circulation cores.

Utilisation (of space)
The quantification of physical presence in workspace over a given period.

Virtual office
The use of a formal office address without access to workspace.

Wellbeing or wellness
The state of being and feeling healthy and happy across a broad range of considerations.

Workplace
The entire domain in which work is undertaken, including physical, digital and human structures and processes.

Worksetting
An installation within workspace in which any form of work is undertaken.

Workspace
The physical and/or digital domain within the workplace in which work is undertaken.

Further reading

The following books offer insight on many of the themes contained in this book. We've skipped the area of leading change as there's a whole library of material available on the subject.

Tim Allen et al., *Working Without Walls: An Insight Into Transforming The Government Workplace* (London: DEGW, 2004).

Rianne Appel-Meulenbroek and Vitalija Danivska (eds), *A Handbook of Theories on Alignment Between People and the Office Environment* (London: Routledge, 2021).

Derek Clements-Croome (ed.), *Creating the Productive Workplace* (London: Routledge, 2021).

Frank Duffy, *Work and the City* (London: Black Dog, 2008).

Joanna Eley and Alexi F. Marmot, *Understanding Offices* (London: Penguin, 1995).

Nicola Gillen, *Future Office: Next-Generation Workplace Design* (London: RIBA, 2019).

Nicola Gillen and Richard Pickering, *Re-working the Workplace: Connecting People, Purpose and Place* (London: RIBA, 2023).

Kursty Groves and Will Knight, *I Wish I Worked There: A Look Inside the Most Creative Spaces in Business* (London: John Wiley & Sons, 2010).

Kursty Groves and Oliver Marlow, *Spaces for Innovation: The Design and Science of Inspiring Environments* (London: Frame, 2016).

Barry Haynes, *Corporate Real Estate Asset Management: Strategy and Implementation* (London: Routledge, 2017).

Bridget Hardy et al., *Working Beyond Walls: The Government Workplace as an Agent of Change* (London: DEGW/Office of Government Commerce, 2008).

Andy Lake, *Beyond Hybrid Working: A Smarter & Transformational Approach to Flexible Working* (London: Routledge, 2023).

Andy Lake, *Smart Flexibility: Moving Smart and Flexible Working from Theory to Practice* (Farnham: Gower, 2013).

Sheila Liming, *Office* (London: Bloomsbury, 2020).

Ana Martins, *Where We Work: Design Lessons from the Modern Office* (London: Frame, 2021).

Jeremy Myerson and Philip Ross, *Unworking: the Reinvention of the Modern Office* (London: Reaktion, 2022).

Nigel Oseland, *Beyond the Workplace Zoo* (London: Routledge, 2021).

Nigel Oseland, *A Practical Guide to Post Occupancy Evaluation and Researching Building User Experience* (London: Routledge, 2023).

Robert Propst, *The Office: A Facility Based on Change* (Elmhurst: The Business Press, 1968).

Neil Usher, *The Elemental Workplace* (London: LID Publishing, 2018).

Neil Usher, *Elemental Change* (London: LID Publishing, 2020).

Juriaan van Meel, Yuri Martens and Herman Jan van Ree, *Planning Offices: A Practical Guide for Managers and Designers* (London: Laurence King Publishing, 2010).

Printed in the United States
by Baker & Taylor Publisher Services